Faint Not

Faint Not

Twelve Brief Meditations on the Word of God

Steven DeLay

WIPF & STOCK · Eugene, Oregon

FAINT NOT
Twelve Brief Meditations on the Word of God

Wipf & Stock
An Imprint of Wipf and Stock Publishers
199 W. 8th Ave., Suite 3
Eugene, OR 97401

www.wipfandstock.com

PAPERBACK ISBN: 978-1-6667-3826-1
HARDCOVER ISBN: 978-1-6667-9874-6
EBOOK ISBN: 978-1-6667-9875-3

04/18/22

Endurance is the queen of the virtues.

—SAINT JOHN CHRYSOSTOM

Contents

Part 1

Chapter 1

The Promise of Eternal Life

WHAT GREAT YEARNING HAS God laid on your heart? What task do you know, however inchoately, is yours to complete? What work is yours to finish? What journey, with a sense of inescapability you cannot ignore, is yours to undertake? Until you begin, each passing day will be another one for which, as we regrettably are too often able to say, "Today, nothing happened."[1] But begin and truly seek out that to which you are called to do, and you will come to learn who you are by accomplishing whatever God has wished to accomplish through you. And whatever it may be, in doing so, more importantly, you inevitably will learn what truly is life's greatest task of all: the task of responding to God's promise of eternal life.

In this life, it is very easy as a matter of habit, however unnatural, to only set our minds on the things of time, on all of the concerns and cares never ceasing to assail us. Time itself becomes routine, hollowed out of anything beyond the fleeting satisfaction accompanying the fulfillment of the transitory concerns responsible for prompting and compelling our attention. Time is thus

1. For a characterization of the everydayness revelation interrupts, see Marion, *D'Allieurs*, 37–61.

3

tedium, a toilsome procession of vacuous desire. Fixing us within the unceasing flux of what is life's familiar wheel of discontent, desire continually brings forth a series of concerns that weigh on us. When desire conjures up that with which you must contend, perhaps you attempt to stifle its claim by pushing it out of your mind, but alas, it is of no use; for eventually, consigning it to the margins of your heart fails, the desire prevails, and, held captive to it, you finally turn to meet what you wish didn't preoccupy you. You tell yourself that if it must be so, at least facing what concerns you might this time prove itself worthwhile. But experience has been a cruel teacher, so having been here before, you know it won't be. The concern is simply a task, an oppressive necessity, something merely to be dealt with and forgotten, because it won't provide any gratification outside the fleeting contentment of having at last exiled it. To be sure, there is always a faint consolation in knowing you will be rid of it once the desire is satiated, a premonition of the momentary sweetness that awaits when priding yourself for having addressed it. And so, voilà! Now you've done it and you're finished—the concern that had worried you is obliterated, consigned to the heap of everything else no longer worth remembering. And like a thorn in your side removed, there is relief. But desire is cruel, and so what you had dreaded most of all now overtakes you. For just as soon as the worry of this initial concern abates, here another one rises up to take its place. The time of routine, then—this time of seamless concern—you sigh, is what it is, an always already burdened time.[2] For no matter what at the particular moment happens to matter next, the concerns materialize as quickly as those

2. Schopenhauer is recognized for having underscored the insatiability of desire. Yet, Plato had noted it also, terming it "by nature insatiable" in the *Republic*, 442a. John Locke, for his part, identified it too, noting in *An Essay Concerning Human Understanding* the "*uneasiness of desire*" (Taylor, *Sources of the* Self, 170; italics in the original). Heidegger, in turn, more or less following Kierkegaard, later radicalized the insight by characterizing the fundamental attunement of existence as being one of anxiety, a concerned time that feels itself too burdened by its own care (see Carlisle, "Kierkegaard and Heidegger"; Kierkegaard, *Concept of Anxiety*, 52–80). For an unmatched explication of the way in which this resulting anxious time is a tormented time, one grace alone can alleviate, see Gramont, *Le discours*, 8–17.

before have since evaporated. Even if one never dares confess it to others, one comes to see what one knows others feel too. Buried deep in your restless heart is a painful acknowledgment that all these desires are vanity. You are sentenced to repeat, day after day, the same routine, the same cycle of worry and empty action.[3] You would disassociate yourself from it all if you could, but doing so is impossible. Desire never ceases, and so you must remain hostage to what you accordingly find yourself doing, no matter how much part of you may not want to do it. Oh, the despair of routinized time! The sadness of knowing that each day nothing happens or will happen, nothing but the fact that you once again have attended to what you feel does not matter! Death itself might seem a blessing if only, for reasons you don't fully comprehend, you didn't fear it. This is the death of desire, the living death of a time that feels the immensity of its own banality. There could be comfort in the solidarity of knowing others feel it also, but torment is torment, even if it is shared. There could be comfort in knowing that death is not as yet here, that there is still time, if only time itself, with its great tedium and merciless restlessness, were not the enemy! To wish perhaps that you were dead while simultaneously fearing death itself—this is the cruelty of the concerns of time, the worries of this today on which, just like any other before it, nothing happened.

True, of course you don't feel this way always. Sometimes it is possible for you to convince yourself that your heart has been deceitful, that you have been taken in by an illusion. Not everything, after all, you recognize, is banal. Who would deny this life offers its genuine consolations? When you are honest, though, this is the ugliest truth of all! For this time, this time of unrelenting concern, is itself destined ultimately to take away this cherished something from you. Money or fame, power or glory, admiration or influence, a career, a love, it doesn't matter what exactly—it, too,

---

3. If forgetting God is evil, so then is one's resulting time. Simone Weil describes such temporality as monotonous: "Monotony of evil: never anything new, everything about it *equivalent*. Never anything real, everything about it imaginary . . . Real evil is gloomy, monotonous, barren, boring" (Weil, *Gravity and Grace*, 119–20).

like all the things you would not despair to lose, shall succumb to time eventually, and so pass away. What a thought! How cruel, you think to yourself, that the one thing that excepts itself from the rest of life's banality must be stolen from you too, by the very time in which you are permitted to so briefly savor it. Perhaps you tell yourself such impermanence is cause for gratitude, that it only resolves you to appreciate all the more what you have while you still can, knowing as you do that it will one day be gone. Time takes what it gives—that is the way of the world, you admit. Yes, perhaps the only thing to be learned here, you think, is the necessity of accepting the inevitable dissolution of what you hold most dear. And so, you resign yourself to the apparent fact that life is, to borrow Kierkegaard's turn of phrase, a dark saying, for what more can one do?

This, then, is the despair of time. For it is difficult to decide in your moments of quiet contemplation which apparent fate is worse: that everything is merely a ceaseless procession of frivolity, or that the one thing which is otherwise must itself inevitably be taken from you. Either way, time seems to be laughing at you. There is nothing you can do about it but resign yourself to time, which increasingly callouses you to the pit it has already burrowed within you. Your sigh, although you may not yet appreciate it to be so, is the expression of the melancholy it is, because it is the expression of the time that feels itself leading only to death. If you cannot be through with desire, you know that eventually, time will be through with you, and death, so you think, will annihilate everything that had once been and will then be gone.

And so, the rebel in you is born. True, time may laugh at you. But you shall laugh back in its face. For something dark has chilled your heart as the ultimate "revenge against time"[4] is conceived within you. What better revenge against the injustice of time than to spite it by wallowing in its futility, willfully subjecting yourself to its sorrows and regrets, emptying yourself entirely of any hope besides that of having the last word in reply to it? Time will one day be finished with you, to be sure, but in the meantime, until

4. Nietzsche, *Thus Spoke Zarathustra*, §251.

your very last defiant breath is drawn, you will refuse to find any consolation but that of clinging to time, no matter how pathetic a gesture you know that to be. Defiance, you decide, henceforth will be your daily bread.

Consequently, though perhaps it may not be so obviously at first, the life you lead disfigures itself, intoxicated as it is by the unbridled attempt to stupefy itself through the excesses of exhausted desire. Do what you will, it makes no difference. The results are always the same. Paradoxically, this frustrated desire expresses itself most clearly in what others might mistake for passion, the apparent "zest for life," the pursuit of the novel and unexpected, in the perpetual striving to find ways to somehow relieve itself of its own resentment, of its torment over knowing that no matter what it does, nor with how much zeal it does so, life still remains finally beholden to the time mocking it. With each passing day in which nothing happens besides the failed pursuit of a satisfaction that such voraciousness knows to be responsible for mutilating the heart of the one who deploys it, time passes, the dread deepens, and the reality of rebellion's futility grows stronger.

Ah! But for you, the rebel, this futility becomes its own nourishment. Frustration is its own delight. In fact, if this feverish desire is sufficiently developed, it even prides itself on its capacity to take pleasure in its own disillusionment. More money, more power, more success, more admiration, more adventure—this desire knows deep down that attaining more does not matter, for this very thirst for the *more* is precisely what underscores the abyss from whence it originated, that desire responsible for having ejected you on the quest of finding new ways to enflame it.[5] In this

---

5. In the Scriptures, desire is routinely equated to thirst. It can take two distinct forms, each inexhaustible. On one hand, there is the thirst for worldly things, a carnal thirst. On the other, there is a spiritual thirst, the desire for God. For an analysis exploring how desiring God is itself to be understood as a thirst—a thirst, for example, exemplified by the Samaritan woman at the well in John's Gospel—see DeLay, *In the Spirit*, 1–19. Recently, Jean-Luc Marion has also taken up the story of the woman at the well in order to illustrate the nature of desiring God (see Marion, *D'Ailleurs*, 221–26). In both instances, it is proper to speak of expansion, for the desire is at once incessant and increasing. Unlike, however, the excess of the desire for worldly things, which ends in

desire that has resolved to avenge itself against time by satisfying itself with nothing else but what time itself has to offer, you discover, as you suspect others have too, that in willing a mastery over time, you have only willed your own torment. And yet, this is such desire's crown jewel, its deepest satisfaction, its stronghold—to knowingly ravish itself in continually willing its own futility. After all, what else is to be done? Thus, in the progressively rarer moments of quiet contemplation in which you ponder what you've become, of where your desire had led you, there is still that same time leading to death, and nothing more.

But there is an objection! And a fair one at that. For the demonic figure just described, you concede, may well be an apt description of some. But it is not representative of you. In the world, such people exist—those who have abandoned all hope and chosen to torment themselves in a silo of spite against time. But you, so you say—you are not so. You do not rage against time. In fact, truth be told, your life is rather unremarkable, even tepid. Time, you think, is your friend. Your existence is not one of rebellious fury but rather mundane contentment. There are anxieties and worries and concerns, yes (for those are inevitable, you will concede), but this thirst for revenge against time, this despair just described—you know nothing of that. Although others may have perfected their rebellion against time in the way mentioned, not you. For you, each day passes without anything of serious consequence. It is the life of the perfectly banal, just the daily routine of your ordinary affairs, and that is it. Perhaps you even take comfort in this, for the banality lulls you into feeling that there is no danger. There is still more time, you think, and although time is impermanent, enough of it still remains for you not to be concerned with this fact. You have nestled yourself into the bosom of time, as if time will never come to an end for you.

---

emptiness, the desire for God, while inexhaustible, leads to fulness. The Septuagint highlights the distinction between these two desires when it says, "The ungodly were judged in wrath and tormented, thirsting in another manner than the just" (Wis 11:9).

Take as an example the man of science. This man is a professor at a respected university, a husband and father. He has a large salary and savings for retirement. He travels the world sharing his research with others. He teaches his classes, mentors his students, and publishes his papers. He is a distinguished man of learning, a man who has left his mark on his field of inquiry. He is even a model citizen. He votes in elections, follows the news. If you should ask him, he will have a sensible view on most matters of the day. When he comes home from work, dinner is waiting. He watches some television and discusses the events of the day with his wife. At night in bed, he reads biographies or other works of vague intellectual interest. He pays his taxes. He even gives to charity. His life, thus, has unfolded in strict accordance with the ordinary stages of life those of the world take for granted to be the natural progression of existence. His children are now grown up; they have begun to make their way in the world as well, and so now he is a grandfather. This causes some alarm, as he must admit to himself when he is being honest. He knows, after all, that this means that his own time is short, that soon death will come for him, as it has for his parents. But he puts this out of mind, pressing deeper each day into the tasks of his work and family life. If he is lucky, he thinks, he may still yet contribute something genuinely groundbreaking to his field, perhaps even win some sort of medal for it. And when he is dead, his colleagues will remember him as a productive fellow, even a good man. Perhaps the university will endow a chair in his name or name a lecture hall in his honor. There will be a funeral where those who knew him eulogize the various things he accomplished. If fortune truly smiles on him, his life's research will be used for further investigations. He will leave a legacy, and he takes comfort in knowing this.

But ask this man about God, and he will state he has no strong opinion. Such a matter is beyond us, he will say. He trusts only what he can see and hear. Anything else is hocus-pocus and of no concern to him. God for him is a matter of indifference. And so, from childhood to adolescence, from adolescence to young manhood, from young manhood to middle age, and from middle age to old age, he has remained sensate, exclusively focused on the things of this life: his career, his family, his hobbies. But what now, now that time is finally running out? Death is closer than ever before, and he knows it. Sometimes it fills him with conscious dread. When he was young, of course, he knew he would one day die. But death was not so proximate. In a way, time itself felt to be unending. There was no reason to consider it seriously. Everyone dies, he knew, and of course he would one day die too, but in a way, death was an abstraction, and so he lived as if he would never die, as if time would always be there, as if one day it would not take away everything he had built and acquired. Like, then, the man who built a greater barn to house his treasure (Luke 12:18), he has paid no concern to eternity, no concern to God.[6] What, then, of this

---

6. In Division Two of *Being and Time*, Heidegger famously notes the tranquilizing effect of an inauthentic understanding of death, one in which we content ourselves with the placating thought that everyone dies (Heidegger, *Being and Time*, 298 [§51]). Heidegger's account of how an authentic understanding of death individuates us remains incomplete, however, for it omits the essential—namely, eternity and the judgment of God. Death matters not simply because it structures our possibilities in time but because it reminds us of the inescapability of God, that what we will have made of our temporal possibilities will determine our standing in eternity. Although the division between Athens and Jerusalem is in many ways an oversimplification, invoking it here is illuminating. Ultimately, Paul's speech to Agrippa gives far more to think about death than does the tome of the philosopher of the Black Forest.

Of course, there is a long, rich, and intricate story to be told regarding theology's reception of Heidegger's philosophy. Should theology embrace or spurn Heidegger's fundamental ontology, beginning with its existential analytic of *Dasein*? Such was the choice facing theologians in the immediate years following *Being and Time*'s publication. A variety of widely different responses took shape. In keeping with the example of Tertullian, who saw a stark divide between Athens and Jerusalem, some—such as Barth—viewed Heidegger's fundamental ontology as inherently irrelevant (even hostile) to theology, and hence unworthy of comment. Adopting the opposite extreme, some—such as Bultmann—happily appropriated Heidegger's existential analytic for the purposes of theology. Others, however, took a more measured approach, neither wholly rejecting it (as Barth) nor unreservedly accepting it (as Bultmann). Dietrich Bonhoeffer, for example, while crediting Heidegger as the first philosopher to work out the "problem of coordinating act and being" as best as philosophy is able, nevertheless maintained that Heidegger's philosophy found its fulfillment only within a theological framework (Dietrich Bonhoeffer, qtd.

man, our successful scientist, our husband and father, our model citizen? Despite the admitted charms and overall tranquility of his life, is not this figure one of despair? To be sure, he may not rage against time, but he has entrusted himself to it all the same.

If Pelagius was right to characterize the reprobate mind as that which has no desire to know God,[7] then although such a one is certainly not a representation of the demonic, he is nevertheless lost, lost in the mist of time. He may not be what the world considers an overtly wicked man, but because he has put his trust wholly in time rather than in God, he at last has been forced to face the reality of having lived as he has chosen to live: "Vanity is everything that some day comes to an end."[8] Ignoring God, he has spent his time sunk in the matters of time. He has chosen to know only creation but not the Creator. He has lived comfortably and bountifully, grateful for the possessions he has but never mindful of the one who has brought him into being, the one who has given him everything he has received. He has never recognized his life to be a gift from God. And so, nearing the end of his time, he has no relationship with God, and hence, no hope. Existing solely for time, he is cut off from eternity, a miserable condition owing to having lived a life in which "dead things were his hope" (Wis 13:10).[9] Life is drawing ever closer to an end, and soon it will be as if nothing happened—for he has built his house on sand, the sands of time.

What of you, then? For whether you are more like the demonic type who avenges himself against existence by knowingly willing the futility of your own desires purely for that reason, or more like the professor who has lived a charmed, tranquil life, the essential remains. For although you may take comfort in knowing your relative youth means you have more time than the aged

---

in Byle, *Bonhoeffer's Christological Reinterpretation*, 19). For an illuminating study of Heidegger's profound influence on Bonhoeffer, see Byle, *Bonhoeffer's Christological Reinterpretation*, 61–96.

7. Pelagius, *Commentary*, 67.

8. Pelagius, *Commentary*, 110.

9. Unless noted otherwise, all citations of the Old Testament, including the Apocrypha, are taken from the Septuagint.

professor, still each day passes under the black sun of vanity. Nothing happens, because life for you does not as yet unfold in light of the promise of eternal life.

But why not? When you reflect on your station, you must admit that you know something of eternity. You know you are mortal, that one day you will die. Perhaps part of you wishes that this was not so, that you could live forever, that you could enjoy the things of time that give you satisfaction for exactly what they are, but only in perpetuity. But this is your problem. You know it is not to be so. Because you do not yet know God, you cling to time, to the illusory hope that even though everything you have is slipping away, existence makes no further demand of you, requires no acknowledgement beyond that of accepting the transience of your life. This, if you are honest, is why you must put God out of your mind. For God has not called you merely to accept the fleetingness of time. He has called you to recognize the vanity of all things, so that you might finally live in the light of eternity. God, in short, has not demanded that you simply resign yourself to the impermanence of this life. No, he demands that you live it by preparing yourself for eternity. And this is what you are still unwilling to do. And so, beneath the tranquil veneer of your daily life's banality, at heart, you see, you are still a rebel. For you put all your efforts into the tasks of this life and its time, paying no concern to how such efforts will be viewed by God on the day of judgment. You have decided to become what time will make of you, rather than become what God wills you to become through the promise of eternal life.

It is not difficult to show that your use of time is rooted in ignoring God's claim on you. The aged professor, after all, could very well have been a professor while still acknowledging eternity and God. From God's point of view, perhaps there is nothing wrong with being a professor. The rebellion in question does not consist in being a professor per se but rather in willing to be one without ever caring whether or not this is truly God's intention for you. The same applies just the same to others. To be a mother, father, banker, teacher, lawyer, insurance agent—none of these things are crimes in themselves. But choosing to be so without ever doing so in light of God's calling for you—that is a crime. The crime consists in desiring to be who you are without ever acknowledging whether this is what God has truly willed you to be. You have made your life yours alone, as if God—and eternity—has made no claim on you and your time. This is why, no matter what exactly they have chosen to become, those who have lived solely for time, rather than for God, instinctively bristle at the idea that they will be held accountable for how they have spent their time. If becoming what they have by their choices were not truly first rooted in the willful choice to discount God's attitude toward those choices, then there would be no reason to resist the notion that God will judge them in light of what they have done with their time through those choices. "In my Father's house are many mansions: if *it were* not *so*, I would have told you. I go to prepare a place for you" (John 14:2, italics in the original). There are many mansions in heaven, Christ says. Room enough for all the world's bankers, teachers, and salesmen, but only if, in willing to be what they've become, they ultimately willed to become what God willed. That one is a salesman does not in itself decide whether one has lived in light of the promise of eternal life. But the fact that one man does not fear to be judged for having become so, while the other does, tells you all you need to know. Even in the most mundane of worldly decisions, eternity intervenes, for when time is over, you will be asked to account for how you lived it, whether for yourself, in denial of your Creator, or for him, in light of the promise of eternal life.

Now imagine that our professor of science is instead a professor of history. He knows history, for he reads it, he studies it, he contemplates it, he writes and lectures about it. From the world's perspective, the distinguishing mark of greatness is to leave a mark on history. Hence, this professor of history, while a man of history insofar as he spends his life thinking about it, remains a spectator. He reads and writes about what great men of the past have done, yet he himself is not great. He might resent his own life for this reason, wishing that he himself had become something great, had accomplished in his own life something worthy of the pages he reads. Or perhaps he lives vicariously through those of whom he reads, as if he makes himself party to greatness by admiring it as he does. He may not be exceptional, he concedes to himself, but he appreciates the exceptional, understands the exceptional, values the exceptional.

But this is all confusion! God does not demand what the world considers the exceptional. In the spirit, the exceptional is simply living before God each day such that, when time is over, one will be able to honestly answer for each of those days. That becoming who you are should unfold in the promise of eternal life accounts for the simplicity, the nobility, of being human. This is why those who do not yet heed the call of Christ in their life inevitably fall into such confusion. They make the mistake of thinking that life is about attaining what will vindicate their use of its time. The thirst for accomplishments betrays the vanity of that very pursuit. Become the world's richest man, and in eternity your great fortune is nothing. In a way, and for this reason, each man dies penniless. Become the world's most famous man, and in eternity your renown is nothing. Become the most powerful man, and in eternity you will still bow to Christ. How many humble people have entered the kingdom of heaven, completely unknown to the world, forgotten by history? We read of great emperors and kings, of explorers and inventors, of revolutionaries and reformers. And yes, they accomplished something in this world with the time they were given. But if they did not do what they did in light of the promise of eternal life, then eternity negates whatever they accomplished in this life. "Enter through the narrow gate. For wide is the gate and broad is the road that leads to destruction, and many enter through it. But small is the gate and narrow the road that leads to life, and only a few find it" (Matt 7:13–14). Christ did not say the way that leads to eternal life is narrow because it is reserved for those who become great in the world's eyes. He said the way is narrow because so few ever recognize that true greatness is doing what God wills, no matter how humble and otherwise insignificant your station in life may appear in the eyes of the world.[10] You

10. A simple verse from Sirach, or Ecclesiasticus, is telling in this regard: "Great men, and judges, and potentates, shall be honoured; yet is there none of

may not accomplish anything in time worthy of mention in the annals of history, but your name will nevertheless be written in the book of life. For the world might not have known you, but Christ knows you.

As for the man of the world who accomplished great things—the Napoleon or the Einstein—he has his name secured in man's written history. But did he thereby know God? That is the essential. Hannibal scaled the Alps by elephant. That we know. But by doing so, does it follow that he became worthy of ascending the mount of Zion? Copernicus studied the order of heavenly hosts. That we know. But by doing so, does it follow that the motions of his own heart were pleasing to God? Picasso painted what his muse gave him to see. That we know. But by doing so, does it follow that the canvas of his heart was unblemished before God? Napoleon crowned himself emperor. That we know. But in doing so, does it follow that he will receive a crown of glory in the kingdom of heaven? Alexander conquered all the kingdoms of man. That we know. But in doing so, does it follow that he will inherit the new heavens and earth? Sinatra crooned beautifully on the world's stage. That we know. But in doing so, does it follow that he shall sing with the angels? Admittedly, the secrets of the heart are unknown to everyone save God, but if common sense is not entirely inappropriate here, if anything, it stands to reason that the greater the things one accomplishes in this world and the more one is extolled by history for them, the more likely it is one will be viewed as a failure in the eyes of eternity. What appeared to matter in time to men does not thereby matter in eternity to God. You alone know whether what you are currently striving to accomplish with the time given to you will be worthy of eternity.

At the end of the day—that is to say, on the last day—eternity will not have demanded that you accomplish what the world conceived of greatness. It will rather judge simply whether or not you willed the good, whatever that may (or may not) have accomplished in the light of the world. For in eternity, your judge will not be the witness of others but God alone. This is the mistake

them greater than he that feareth the Lord" (Sir 10:24).

those who live solely to accomplish things here in time fail to understand. Seeking the glory that comes from men, they spurn the glory that comes from God only. Seeking the witness of men, they ignore the true "cloud of witnesses" (Heb 12:1), the hosts of heaven looking down upon man. What a pity! To stake life on what is only passing away, to stake success on what other men deem estimable, while neglecting what success means in the eyes of God—that life be lived with your eyes fixed on the promise of eternal life.

How, you ask, does this eternal promise unfold in time? If it is ever to unfold, it will only be by heeding not just the call that originates from the world but instead the call from within, the call originating nearer to you than you are to yourself,[11] the call of Christ calling you to eternal life in him. This is faith. Not a matter of mere belief. Not just a matter of propositional assent. Faith, and the life it leads in the course of time, is trust, fidelity, loyalty, commitment. In short, it is a life that perseveres in the expectation of God's faithfulness, a temporality no longer in which you are ejected outside of yourself—hurtling toward some vanity that will only disappointment you and ultimately fade away anyway—but in a temporality sustained by the fullness of eternity, of God's promise that you will find yourself in him, and through him alone. This, and this alone, is time's true task.

11. Augustine, *Confessions*, 3.6.11. Augustine's exact phrase is "more intimate to me than I am to myself."

Chapter 2

Here Are My Mother and Brothers

IF THERE WERE ANY denying that existence is a mystery, do not the circumstances of our very births testify to the fact that our own origin resides outside us? That, finding ourselves unable to orient ourselves intelligibly within time apart from him, God calls to us from beyond it? Everyone is born, to be sure, yet nobody can remember his own birth. From this very beginning, one that will never be a conscious past as it was never first a retainable present, our existence is suspended between a past forever escaping it and a future inexorably exceeding it. On all sides there stretches out an indeterminateness defying our comprehension, shrouding both the birth and death that will eventually constitute the bookends to our time. To be born, among other things, thus, is to experience our powerlessness to exercise any sovereign authority or mastery over our own being, which, though easy to forget, has been received, as a gift, from elsewhere than ourselves. And when we do reach an age of self-consciousness, in which memory has successfully established us within the horizon of recollection, this origin, our natural birth, is something that always remains inaccessible to us, except through the testimony of others who witnessed or experienced it for themselves. Hence, time and testimony are interwoven. For the statements and explanations of others are what assist us above all in first recognizing what it means to exist, to find ourselves present to the world by way of a birth itself eluding us, an irretrievable and originary event which has not left even the scantest of a trace—since, as we cannot at all recall it or ever hope to recall it, we are straightaway made to understand that we will never be present to it.[1] That for us time should be opened by an event that will never present for us is consequently the first indication, though by no means the last, that our destiny lies beyond time. Calling us into being through a birth we cannot recall, God thereby has always already set the stage for our second birth, when, if we so choose, we are born again, not in time but now in him. What a marvelous mystery of time that this second birth alone should be the first and only one we initiate and remember! In this way, this second birth supersedes its forerunner, a fitting verification that eternity itself must supersede time.[2]

For the Enlightenment tradition of modern philosophy inaugurated by Descartes, radicalized by Kant, and then further deepened by the idealists, such as Hegel, Schelling, Fichte, and others, it is our human autonomy—the capacity to self-regulate our life in accord with reason, to give ourselves the law—that is thought to define our dignity. To live rationally in this way is to "lead a life," to order existence in time in light of the autonomous capacity to set our own purposive ends for ourselves. It goes without saying that in this view, God effectively is neutralized, excised, and purged from the economy of human willing and desire. The resulting picture of maturation into adulthood consists in the task of casting off the last vestiges of religious superstition.[3]

And yet, to have spoken here of a second birth in the manner we have, of birth distinct from our first natural birth—is this not to

1. Claude Romano, for one, has discussed the originary structure of birth extensively (see Romano, *There Is*, 26–66).

2. For a beautiful meditation on this immemorial presence of God, who transcends our living memory, see Chrétien, *Unforgettable*, 40–77.

3. For a statement illustrative of this modern consciousness defining itself in terms of autonomous reason, see Pippin, *Idealism as Modernism*, 417–50.

invoke, perhaps unwittingly, the same figure of autonomy characterizing the modern, rational identity? For if our first birth bringing us into the world transcends our powers of self-sovereignty, is not the second birth, the birth into life in God, a birth which originates in us, with the decision to respond to God, and which therefore constitutes an exercise of our own willing—and hence, a representative instance of the aspiration to govern ourselves, to master ourselves, to reign supreme over one's own future? If this were so—if being born again in God were to be equated with an exercise of autonomous willing—perhaps then it would indeed make better sense simply to dispense with the notion of a second birth in Christ. It would make sense to purge such a conception of any residue of heteronomy and speak instead of a birth into adulthood, an initiation into the life of autonomous human reason—a life said to distill the essence of self-determining free agency, by first having eliminated all lip service to the law of God, which might otherwise have been thought to bind us as human beings.

But this understanding of the second birth, the birth of which Christ speaks with Nicodemus, is a misunderstanding. When the Spirit of God blows, as it did on Nicodemus, calling us to be born again, it is not the world spirit of Hegel that encounters us but rather the Holy Spirit, he that speaks by addressing us individually, not in reference to our place within the rational unfolding of world history but rather in terms of our personal vocation to become a son of God and the calling to inherit the kingdom of heaven. To respond to such a call affirmatively requires an act of our submission. It is to exercise the will, to be sure. But this act of freedom is an act of willing only insofar as it submits its will to Christ. It is not to give ourselves the law but to submit to God's law. Hence, it is not at all a decision to lead a life in light of the dictates of an autonomous reason, with a secular eye solely to the things of this world. It is a commitment to lead a life in light of the Word, who, directing us where he in turn pleases, accordingly sets the eyes of our heart on the promise of eternal life.[4]

4. For a further explication of the way in which the heart has its own senses, see DeLay, *In the Spirit*, 66–82. This is a biblical theme, one particularly salient

When, then, this Spirit of God blows and one responds by being born into it, one does not become a citizen of autonomous reason's cosmopolitan world order. One becomes a pilgrim on the earth, someone whose home lies wholly beyond the world. This is why the second birth can rightly be likened to a kind of death. For to be born again is to die to the world and all the transient things that had once captivated us about it. In short, the old man, the man who had thought himself to be an adult, an autonomous man of the world, recognizes finally that he in fact has not yet known life—true life, eternal life in Jesus Christ. And so, when this old man dies, the new man is born. At last, here lies true freedom, not the specious sort of modern autonomous reason but rather the freedom liberated from its own former self-imposed tutelage by emptying itself into the Spirit of God, thereby passing from death to life.

Here, we have come to the essential. For if the history of modern philosophy's various treatises has the habit of tempting us to believe that the issues of life can be adequately resolved by thinking about what lies on their pages, the words of Christ say otherwise. These latter words are different. Addressing us in a way that eliminates any possibility of compartmentalization or distance, these words—words which Christ says are the words of life—do not address you as a reader or a thinker. At least, not only so. Addressing you as a single human being, as an individual before God, they address you so as to make you face the choice of whether to continue on as a child of time, as a man of the world, or whether instead you will be born again. Do you yourself know this life yet, and this second birth? Or do you still toil under the tutelage of your own will, a slave to your desires and ends? Are you still an aimless child of time, laboring under the worldly burden of a life that knows nothing but the time leading it to death? Do you know the words of life, or are you still enamored with the dead words of the philosopher's pages?

Truth be told, we have so many motivations for choosing to overcomplicate what is in fact simple, which is why, in the last analysis, the words of Kant, Hegel, Fichte, or Schelling, however

in the Song of Songs, as shown by Chrétien, *Symbolique du corps*, 15–44.

brilliant or otherwise illuminating they may be, are not alive. And nor are we alive if we continue to use them to stifle the word of God. For they are mere dead words. Yes, only the words of Christ are life. The former words, which give voice to what the world considers to be wisdom, are words of curiosity and amusement—even, perhaps, of learning, which has its own form of seriousness. But only these other words, those of Christ, are the most serious of all words, for they alone are the words of life. It would be ludicrous to live a life seriously thinking that one's life will be brought into judgment by Kant or Hegel. They are mere men. If, then, understandably, nobody rightly fears that his life will be judged in accord with the words Kant or Hegel uttered, this is because Kant and Hegel themselves, just as everyone else, for that matter, will be judged as individual human beings by Christ's words. Man may think. He may write. He may promulgate his various systems. But in the end, all this intellectual labor is expended to erect a house built on sand if it mistakes itself for somehow being capable of substituting itself for the word of God. For every word, every thought, and every deed will be judged by Christ, not systems crafted by men who, for whatever their reasons, chose to disregard him. This consideration alone demonstrates the foolishness of anyone's staking his self-understanding on such systems. Proclaiming to speak from the fount of reason, such systems forget that everyone, even those who invent such systems, will be answerable to God ultimately. What, then, could be more irrational than this—than an individual who, touting such systems to be the exemplars of human reason, thereby ignores his own personal condition as an individual before God?

At bottom, it is this eternal accountability that offends the rebel, the autonomous man, who, desiring to lead his own life in accordance with his own law, bristles at the God to whom he refuses to acknowledge he must submit. Kant, in emblematic fashion, scoffed at the idea that man is a creature of God. Such a situation, were it the case, he thought, would render man little more than a "pet of God."[5] From the worldly perspective of a dignified man intent upon being answerable to nobody besides himself, this is

5. Pippin, "Seminar 3."

an insult to human nobility, a mockery of man. But what is worse? What more wretched? Humbly accepting that one is a creature of God and thus living a life in submission to God, or ignoring the Creator, and so leading a life as if one were one's own lawgiver? True enough, the autonomous man may console himself in time with the thought that he retains his dignity by refusing to be seen as a pet of God. And yet, in the eyes of eternity, he has become far worse. For now, he is a sort of buffoon or clown! What, after all, could be more comical than the figure of a man who, brought into being by God, squandered all his years on earth, existing day after day as if he were not destined to answer to the very God whom he ignored? Far better to be a pet of God than this man of the world, a clown of time! Viewed from eternity, the man of the world, this man of time, this man of autonomous reason, has settled for an adulthood which really is a stunted childhood. He is like the toddler playing with his toys in the sand box who never realized that what he took to be so serious, so important, were in fact trifles. If such a serious matter can be put in metaphorical illustrations, then yes, as it happens, when it comes right down to it, far better to be a pet of God than the clown on the world stage or the toddler in the sand box!

Is this not why Christ says that in order to enter his kingdom, one must first become a child? This means one must learn humility, must renounce the counterfeit adulthood that had come to define one in the world, must abandon the posture of seriousness and importance that characterizes men of the world who take their being for granted. This is the paradox—that the man who lives for time and for the world, and who thereby disregards God, unwittingly lives as a foolish child when thinking he has become an adult. Only the one who recognizes God and is born again has ripened into maturity through the acknowledgment of eternity, for such is the one who lives his life in time with an eye to God's kingdom. You see, either way, one is a child. Either one exists as a child of time and the world, as a child of one's own desires—in which case one leads a life of specious adulthood, failing to abandon the childishness of one's defiance—or else one matures and is born again, learning obedience and self-dispossession, and becomes a child of God.

In regard to the first birth, the one that brought us into the world, the one that we never remember—and so in a way is as if nothing to us—it is an event for others, for those who saw it or heard about it. Let us focus on the customary case, or at least the ideal one. You come into the world in a delivery room, overseen by a doctor and nurses, who hand you to your jubilant mother. Your mother strokes your face and kisses your forehead, nestling you gently in her arms. In the room is your father, who, in a state of shock and euphoria, can barely believe his eyes. You, his son or daughter, is here, and for him, now life will never be the same. He walks to the bed and leans over, and stares directly into your face. Your cries do not bother him. To the contrary, he finds them endearing. He grasps your tiny hand and tells you, "I love you." When you were a young child, you were told this story, this story of your birth. You were told how much your mother and father loved you, how happy they were to have you. Perhaps they told you stories of what you were like when you were still in the womb, when you would kick inside when your mother ate ice cream, or wriggle when she rubbed her stomach. You do not remember your mother's first kisses and caresses, nor your father's first words to you, but you know of them. You were told so. For a time, perhaps well into your earliest youth, things are tranquil, even comprehensible. These are your parents, you are here in the world, and you like it that way.

In time, however, something changed. For something happened. There came the moment when you first realized your parents are not perfect. That they are human just like everyone else. They do not know everything. They make mistakes. Perhaps they on occasion even do things that are bad. For the very first time in your life, your parents are seen no longer to be more than human. They, too, you now see, are frail beings, struggling like anyone else to find their own way in life. To be sure, you can still look to them for love and support, and even comfort, but it will never be the same. You cannot see them as you once had. The aura of perfection, and the security it had once offered, is gone.

If you were precocious, perhaps you had noted at the time how your own parents must have had an identical epiphany regarding their own parents too. There came a time when your mother and father realized for themselves that their parents were merely human, were not the perfect ones that only the extremely young are able to think their parents are. Your parents, like you now, at some point lost that unquestioned, absolute confidence in their parents, lost that naïve assurance that their parents were flawless. When you thought about this, you realized that such an experience must have been one that your grandparents also had gone through. Maybe you yourself never met your great-grandparents, but having actually met them wasn't necessary to have known that what had just dawned on you was true of them as well. For they were merely human too, which meant that, inevitably, there had come a moment in their early lives when they had come to be seen in the eyes of your grandparents as mortal, as imperfect, as incomplete, as frail. You had thought that you knew perfection—the absolute, the flawless, the omnipotent. And now, in a moment, you had come to see it was not what you had thought. Nobody is so. All the generations are a great chain of imperfection.

And if you were precocious, perhaps this got you to thinking further. If all parents are flawed, if they must one day come to be seen as less than perfect in the eyes of their children, and if such is the case for every generation, what about the first man? You may not have been told the story of Genesis yet, but in principle, thinking as hard as you could as a young child, you could certainly grasp the notion of the first man, Adam. Logically, you knew, there must have been such a man. Who, then, you wondered, was his father, this first man on the earth without any apparent father?

God, you see, is this man's Father. Are you, then, so unlike Adam? Adam was without any earthly father. You have an earthly father. True! But this is a difference that conceals the essential sameness. From the perspective of eternity, whether one is Adam, an orphan, or born into a loving family, one's true Father still is in heaven. This is something the orphan may well come to discover sooner than those who, from an earthly perspective, appear to have the advantage of possessing an earthly father. But eventually, no matter one's particular circumstances, if one is to be born again, it is necessary to acknowledge what the orphan learns sooner—that there indeed is only one Father of us all, God the Father.

If this hard lesson of youth would seem to teach us that there is no such thing as perfection at all—that our parents are merely human—what then are we to make of the Scriptures' repeated invocation of perfection? In his Sermon on the Mount, for instance, the Lord himself enjoins those who hear him to "Be ye perfect, even as your Father in heaven is perfect" (Matt 5:48). If no one is perfect in knowledge or perfect in power, what can these words mean for us? If even our earthly parents are not perfect, how can we ourselves possibly aspire to be perfect as God the Father? In his letter to fellow believers, the apostle James, for his part, discusses this theme of perfection. He does so in the context of desire, or lust, and thus the phenomenon of temptation. Temptation is a word presupposing our choice and freedom. It means we do not have to do what desire might suggest we should. For, no longer handed over to the winds of passion as before, with the new birth, which James himself presupposes his readers have already undergone, a transformation in our economy of desire has been enacted. To begin with, we are to desire good things and to look down upon that which is bad. Thus, there is the matter of valuation. Where before it was natural to give free reign to the yearnings of the heart, no matter what they were, now such desires must be measured in the light of God's law. This is why, as James says, such a life of desire unfolds in accordance with the "law of liberty" (Jas 2:12), the freedom that comes in Christ, whereby the power to resist evil takes shape.[6] An evil thing that lust conceives now appears as a mere temptation rather than a fait accompli. A deed, as James says, is now the expression of a work done in accord with God's law, or else it is not. To be a "doer of the word" (Jas 1:22) is to do what is aligned with God's law, and so to refrain from doing whatever may be opposed to it. Hence, life in the body itself becomes a work of

---

6. This power, the power of righteousness of the Holy Spirit working within us, is discussed in Koci and Alvis, *Transforming the Theological Turn*, 187–202.

patience, a test of faith, for when such temptation comes, there is the choice of whether to fulfill what the lust in question has conceived, or whether to instead summon the power to remain steadfast in the law of liberty, the law of freedom from death and sin that delivers the one who otherwise would be ensnared by not exercising control over his desires. "Count it all joy," then, when such temptation arises, says James, for in abstaining from whatever is evil, one works a perfect work, a deed done in patience. This, in short, is how one escapes from the cycle of lust that had formerly subjugated the one who had not yet been born again. These evil desires, which pass away like the flower of the grass (Jas 1:10; see also Ps 103:15; 1 Pet 1:24), are overcome in the name of perfect desires—that is to say, desires that find their completion in the obedience to the law of liberty empowering one to abstain from them. And when the temptation passes and the evil has been overcome, this desire oriented to God, and its act of patience, is seen to be a perfect work, "perfect and entire," leaving one "wanting nothing" (Jas 1:4). A carnal indulgence brings no lasting satisfaction, because it is transitory and temporal, which is why Isaiah accordingly says there is no rest for the wicked. But a deed done in the law of liberty works abiding joy, for it accomplishes itself in the word of God, which is eternal.

The apostle Peter, continuing this same theme in James, says as much too. In being born again into the Spirit rather than the flesh, the new man "no longer should live the rest of his time in the flesh to the lusts of men, but to the will of God" (1 Pet 4:2). This form of life governed by a will no longer desiring evil, as he notes, appears very strange to those who have not yet been born again—to those, in short, who, not yet knowing the perfect law of liberty, remain enslaved to their evil lusts. "They think it strange," says Peter, "that you run not with them to the same excess of riot, speaking evil of you" (1 Pet 4:4). Here, then, is the great divide. On the one hand, there are those who, still subject to the despair of time and the rule of their lust, cannot thereby know perfection, for they do not yet know the law of liberty. They are not yet doers of the word, and thus they do not know the perfection of which

Christ speaks when he speaks of the Father's perfection. Then there are those who, on the other hand, knowing this transformed desire, this desire delighting itself in the joy of the law of liberty, no longer are subject to the law of sin and death. Renewed in the Spirit, knowing the power of patience and the perfection that comes with it, their deeds produce a satisfaction only attainable in the life of God.

Finally, this is not all. For just as the transformation of desire transforms us inwardly, so it also transforms how others see us and how we see them. Natural understandings of life's relationships are henceforth subordinated to new conceptions, above all those involving family and friendship. In Matthew's Gospel, for instance, we read a record of an incident in which a crowd of people has assembled to listen to Christ. When he has finished with his parable, a listener approaches him to say that Christ's mother and brothers are outside, waiting to speak with him. How does Christ answer? Stretching out his hand, he gestures to all those assembled around him and says, "Behold my mother and my brethren! For whosoever does the will of my Father who is in heaven, the same is my brother, and sister, and mother" (Matt 12:49–50). This is the heart of the previous teaching from the Sermon on the Mount. If everyone must learn in childhood that his mother and earthly father are imperfect, this is because, ultimately, everyone's true father is God the Father. And if our painful childhood realization that our earthly parents are not perfect disappoints or frightens us, this is only because we must learn this hard truth in order that we may in turn learn in what perfection truly consists. Such perfection is to be found in the law of liberty, in the work of patience that delights itself in the will of God, rather than the lusts of men. This is time's teaching, we see—that even our very birth, the first birth having brought us into the world, points us to a fulfillment lying beyond time commencing with our second birth, in the eternal life promised to those who thereby perfect themselves through the desire to seek the Father who is in heaven.

Chapter 3

Deeds Wrought in God

To commit a deed is to be answerable for it. What could be more obvious? The child learns this at home before hearing the lesson repeated by the teacher on the very first day of school. Others have the right to question us, interrogating our motives or aims for doing what we have done, so as to appraise our judgment and character, since, in a way, manifest in the deed itself is the whole being of the one who did so. A deed, thus, expresses the one who does it, which is why it requires a justification in turn. At the risk of stating what is no less obvious, it is the deed that gives rise to the word—or rather, a demand for the word—to the dialogic exchange in which we stand obligated to give an account of ourselves to others, and they to us. Insofar as action entails the responsibility of being answerable for it, everyday life is a place of discourse, which is to say, light. No one is exempted from having to answer to others, except on pain of failing to do what one should, as failing to be answerable to others flouts the social bond knitting us together. This mundane domain of apparent transparency, then, suggests that the everyday interpersonal milieu in which we act and speak is a space of reasons, one of intelligibility and accountability.[1] And yet, it only

1. Steven Crowell, for one, has developed an account of this

appears so. For, supposing that this form of social intelligibility, with its undergirding norms of responsibility and answerability, is asserted to be the ground of itself, is not there at bottom, then, only an abyss? Were this the case, the everyday practice of being accountable to others—this space of reason, judgment, and discourse—would really be a game of frivolity. With God excluded, what initially may have seemed to be a space of light proves, on the contrary, to be one of darkness. A deed must not only oblige us to recognize our responsibility for being answerable to others. Above all, it obliges us to recognize our accountability to God. If, hence, a deed proves itself capable of a justificatory word, this is only because, in having deservedly satisfied others, it first must satisfy God. And how else can this be but if the deed be wrought in God? Our being answerable to others in word derives its ground in the fact of our deed's being accountable to God. This is the error adults make when thinking they are accountable to others only, and not God. They fail to realize that their merely human practice of excusing and condemning, judging and evaluating, remains groundless—or rather, grounded in what they fail to acknowledge grounds it. Any ultimately justifying human word depends on the deed having originated from the Word.

Such is the lesson Nicodemus learned when he came by night to speak with Christ (see John 3:2). And if he came at night seeking clarity about God, this was quite fitting, because he came seeking a way out of the darkness in which he knew himself to be enshrouded, from out of the dark obscurity of a discourse determined by those who spoke of nothing higher than their own judgments and opinions, a discourse that ignored Christ, who is the Word of God. Nicodemus, who was just, knew the Pharisees were not. He knew that in taking themselves to answer only to each other, these others were ignoring their accountability to God. Preferring a mere semblance of responsibility in speaking of one another's deeds as they did, they thereby silenced the Word. Theirs was a sham discourse. For contrary to initial appearances, the everyday space of human

---

dialogic responsibility as Heideggerian authenticity. See Crowell, *Normativity and Meaning*, 214–36.

reason and discourse is, as David notes in the Psalms frequently, not a place of light but of darkness. Too often, human discourse is wicked, since, rather than aiming at truth, as speech should, it perverts itself, reversing its ontological meaning, by instead seeking to conceal or twist the truth with falsehoods. Rather than serving as a tribunal at which we are held accountable for what we have done by being compelled to answer honestly for our deeds, the everyday practice of reason giving deteriorates into a charade whereby one attempts to avoid responsibility, either by answering falsely or not at all.

To return to the preceding analogy, such behavior is like that of the child who refuses to be answerable to his parents or schoolteacher. And if it would be silly for a child simply to pretend his schoolteacher does not exist because he is unwilling to hear what he knows his schoolteacher has to say, is it any less so for the adult simply to pretend that God does not exist? When Christ counsels Nicodemus, he does not appeal to others. He does not refer Nicodemus to their opinion. He does not propose that Nicodemus measure his deeds in light of what they can justify on their terms. Rather, everything about Christ's words refers Nicodemus back to himself, the Word. Christ, whom Nicodemus says everyone recognizes to be a teacher, situates human deeds and words in the far greater light of himself, the Word.

If the kingdom of God of which Christ speaks is the true light, the true realm of intelligibility in which deeds and words are to be measured, it is for this reason that Christ speaks to Nicodemus as a child. For Nicodemus is a man—a learned man, in fact. But in order to teach Nicodemus what he has come seeking to understand, it will be necessary to show Nicodemus that being a man of the world, a man capable of answering to others, is not the essential. To remain wholly subject in this way to the Pharisees, who themselves are mere men, to pretend as if their words and judgments count for more than human words and opinions should, is to ignore the true measure of whether or not a deed has been done in truth. To know this, it will be necessary to assess whether the deed has been wrought in God. And so, immediately, Christ reminds

Nicodemus, who is a man, that he must in fact be born again, must again become a child. For only in recognizing that one is a child of God does one thereby assume true responsibility for one's deeds. "Verily, verily, I say unto you, Except a man be born again, he cannot see the kingdom of God" (John 3:3). What frank, authoritative words. Words a child might hear from a schoolteacher!

The good child, the one who has become a son of God, listens to the teacher. This is what Nicodemus learns. To listen, as Christ says, is to be directed by the Spirit, by the words of God that resound in the obedient heart. As John's Gospel records, the deeds that originate in this obedience—these deeds that express the Spirit that has blown through the heart of the one who listens—are deeds wrought in God. And hence, they are works of light, works that can easily receive a word of justification, if anyone should ask. Just as there is no darkness in God, so there is no darkness in the deeds that are done in him. Being answerable to others is easy, for one has already been answerable to God. And so, naturally, there is nothing evil to conceal.

In his Epistle to the Colossians, Paul says the same. Being born again, as he explains, is to be obedient, to submit to the Spirit working within the heart, the heart of the one who loves God. Now deeds are no longer measured by the world and its judgments, and how others will perceive them. Instead, deeds at once derive their source and justification in the Word, who has brought them forth. They are the fruits of God, who himself is the vine. As Paul says, "And whatsoever you do, do it heartily, as to the Lord, and not unto men" (Col 3:23). Do what you do heartily, Paul says, which is to say, do it truly, by opening your heart to the commands of God, which are manifest to you through the Spirit speaking within you. Henceforth, such deeds originate in the word of God, in the silent discourse the heart has with Christ. This interiority is something the world's everyday space of accountability omits entirely. But it is absolutely essential to a deed being done in truth. As the Septuagint renders it, David says that the one who has carved out this interiority before God "walks blameless, and works righteousness, [and] speaks truth in his heart. [He is one] who has not spoken craftily with his tongue, neither has done evil to his neighbor, nor taken a reproach against them that dwelt nearest to him" (Ps 14:2–3). Loving God means obeying him—obeying him with an eye to his eventual return. As Paul says again, this time in his Second Epistle to the Thessalonians, "And the Lord direct your hearts into the love of God, and into the patient waiting for Christ" (2 Thess 3:5). Deeds wrought in God open to eternity, not the world, for they manifest the love of the God who has promised us eternal life in him.

Returning to this same theme already articulated in the third chapter of his Gospel, John in his first epistle again iterates the connection between the new birth and obedience. Good deeds—those wrought in God—are works sustaining the new birth, for they are works that work toward entering the kingdom of heaven. As John says, "If you know that he is righteous, you know that everyone that does righteousness is born of him" (1 John 2:29). These works of righteousness do more than render us answerable to others. They establish us in the life of God, whereby we can wait with anticipation of his coming. With our hearts laid bare to him, we have no reason to fear him or to be ashamed. This is what John means when he discusses abiding in God: "Little children, abide in him, that when he shall appear, we may have confidence, and not be ashamed before him at his coming" (1 John 2:28). The next chapter of that same letter makes this clear when John writes, "And he that keeps his commandments dwells in him, and he in him. And hereby we know that he abides in us, by the Spirit which he has given us" (1 John 3:24). And once again, John emphasizes that being born again, which consists in heeding the Spirit shed in our hearts, entails working righteousness: "For this is the love of God, that we keep his commandments" (1 John 5:3). These are works of love, deeds done in the Word.

Nicodemus learns this lesson when he comes to Christ at night. He learns that the new birth is capable of delivering us from the world's darkness, with its evil deeds and false words. For no longer is its sham discourse to be taken seriously. Now that the Word has spoken, the world's notions of responsibility and answerability are exposed to be only apparent. True responsibility consists in being answerable to God, to the Word who has addressed us. Thus, where the first birth brought us into the world and would have left us subject to the hypocrisies and false words of others, this new birth initiates us into the Word. The world is thereby overcome. As John says, "For whatsoever is born of God overcomes the world" (1 John 5:4). Learning what the Pharisees have not yet, Nicodemus is shown that only by hearing the Word of God does one overcome the world's darkness. "Who," John asks, "is he that overcomes the world, but he that believes that Jesus is the Son of God?" (1 John 5:5). Not only does this second birth accomplish an overcoming of the world's false discourse, it opens a new horizon of responsibility entirely, for it opens unto eternal life. John says, "And this is the promise that he has promised us, even eternal life" (1 John 2:25). If true deeds, those done in God, will stand the test of time, this is because they are deeds worthy of Christ, the one who has called us to eternal life. To be sure, mere human words are capable of convincing others that a deed was good when it was in fact bad, that a deed was true when in fact it was false, that a deed was pure when it was in fact murky. This constant possibility of deception essentially characterizes the human milieu of giving and asking for reasons. The inherent susceptibility of the world's discourse to falsehood is why, for example, Christ highlights the distinction between righteous judgment and false judgment. Because not everything is what it appears, as others are capable of deception, one must in turn exercise discernment: "Judge not according to the appearance, but judge righteous judgment" (John 7:24). But with God, no such deception is possible. This is the lesson the man of the world has yet to learn. For deceive everyone you know about what you have done or why you have really done it, and yet you still have not deceived God! God knows the secrets of the heart; he knows whether what you have done was done heartily to him or not.

For this very reason, Paul himself speaks of the day of judgment as one on which we will be judged according to our deeds. As the statement in question is recorded in the Acts, "He has appointed a day, in the which he will judge the whole world in righteousness by that man whom he as ordained; whereof he has given assurance unto all men, in that he has raised him from the dead" (Acts 17:31). Nicodemus, who came at night, had not yet seen Christ risen. But the Spirit had blown on him, and, listening to what it had said to him, he came to speak to the teacher, the Word. Such was Nicodemus's own first step toward eternal life. It is the same step anyone else must make, too, if the new birth of which Christ speaks is ever to occur. Hearing the words of life addressed to it, the heart, spurning the false words of men, must come as a child to the one whose words are true, the Word. It listens to what the Spirit says; it hears that the Spirit is truth. The heart failing to first learn this lesson may be able to go on answering to others in daily life. But all its deeds and words will only be a semblance of truth. This is pharisaical false righteousness, the kind taking itself to be justified only because it justifies itself in the eyes of others. But until the Spirit dwells in the heart, you will never be able to account for yourself to God, for your heart abides in darkness rather than in the light of the Word.

Chapter 4

The Honor That Comes from God Only

IF THE WORLD'S GLORY is passing away, and so ultimately nothing, is not its pursuit foolishness? True enough, very few seem to recognize this is the case, seeing as they dedicate their lives to pursuing such honor anyway. But the fact that the majority of people might not ever recognize the foolishness of striving to attain worldly glory, or at least of admiring it in those who have, does not change the fact that it is foolish. To be sure, it would be a cause for immense despair if such glory—and the honor it is commonly thought to confer—were the only glory and honor this life had to offer. For even assuming this honor of men is in fact something satisfying, as the world suggests, it is nevertheless destined to fade away like the leaf of the tree. And, in any case, it is highly questionable whether such honor is even satisfying for the short duration in which it lasts. But perhaps you scoff. Probably, you are someone personally unacquainted with the honor of men. You are neither famous nor rich, neither powerful nor renowned. Your life in this world passes each day with hardly anyone noticing. Frankly, though it may sound cruel to say, there is no denying your life will be forgotten. For nothing you do will be considered worthy of memory. When you are gone, you will leave no legacy, for during your life, you will never have known the honor that comes from men. And perhaps, then, you think your life would be better if you knew such honor and had such glory. If this is indeed your situation—if to be an obscurity in the eyes of the world destined to be forgotten by time, as if you never lived, as though you never mattered, is to be your fate—then imagine that things were now different for you. Yes, imagine you were now someone truly great in the world's estimation, someone lavished with worldly honors. Imagine, in short, that you are where you currently are, the same person, only now with all the admiration and glory anyone could ever hope to achieve. What a dreadful thought! For what a sorrow it must be to discover at the end of life's struggles and sufferings that everything attained by such means is fleeting glory, this honor that, being of men, was destined to flicker for a moment simply to fade into a dark sea of forgetfulness, to echo pitifully in the empty halls of profane history.[1] What the world conceives as glory, in reality, is far from desirable. After all, who can sincerely deny that worldly accomplishments, if they are remarkable, usually only provoke, if not indifference, the animosity, jealousy, and malice of others? And as for those select few who do happen genuinely to admire rather than envy what one has accomplished, such an audience, however large, could never provide you any enduring satisfaction. Win all the conceivable glory in the world, and there still will be a pit of emptiness in you. If you doubt it, simply look to those who possess all the glory and honor you presently do not,

---

1. Of course, with many Enlightenment thinkers, the goals of fame and gratitude from posterity took on the role of a substitute immortality. One sees this zeal for recognition from future generations, for example, in Diderot, who was deeply preoccupied with the attainment of posthumous fame. He states quite openly that those such as himself who have abandoned the hope of any traditional immortality are right to place their efforts in attaining recognition from the generations to come. The true motivation of such contemporary philosophers of his day, as he writes, is thus posthumous glory: "They flatter themselves that one day we will acclaim them, and that their memory will be forever honoured among men [...] They rejoice in advance in the sweet melody of the distant concert of voices, which will come to celebrate them, and their heart quivers with joy" (Denis Diderot, *Réfutation suivie de l'ouvrage d'Helvétius intitulé De l'homme*, qtd. in Taylor, *Sources of the Self*, 352).

and what do you see? Yes, look to the world's actors, musicians, tycoons, and politicians, and what do you see? If you look honestly, truth be told, you see that these are some of the most miserable people among us. Whatever worldly glory is said to bestow, it isn't happiness. To the contrary, there very likely is no one more discontent than those who, having sought the glory of men and actually attained it, find themselves consequently miserable, for they have not yet learned it is the honor that comes from God only which is truly worthwhile. If, then, we are to consider the question of human nobility, triumph, and honor rightly, this worldly glory, it must be admitted, can safely be put to the side. No, if there is any honor really worth pursuing in this life, it will not be this honor but rather the honor that comes from God only. As the Septuagint states it plainly, "Wisdom is glorious, and never fadeth away; yes, she is easily seen of them that love her and found of such who seek her" (Wis 6:12).

Jesus Christ, the greatest man to ever live, knew something about the world's glory. For this reason, he speaks of the foolishness of not wisely seeking the glory of God but rather the world's sham glory. And despite being the greatest man to walk the earth, he remains the most derided man in the world to this day. Beware, he tells us, what the world takes to be glory! For his very name is but a curse on the lips of hordes of hateful men who are infinitely less great than he! Let us, then, learn from him, the greatest of all men, mocked and scorned by the world his greatness notwithstanding, he who accordingly knew better than anyone that the world's honor and glory are nothing. What does he say of this honor of men, this honor the world so esteems? In a word, Christ dismisses it completely, saying to seek instead the honor that comes from God only (see John 5:44). How pitiful the world's glory must truly be, for the greatest man who ever lived to think so little of it!

Just consider! Who do you think better understands greatness—the perfect man, Jesus Christ, or the collection of actors and musicians and politicians and tycoons upon which the world in each of its generations heaps its honors? Humphrey Bogart, John Belushi, and Sean Connery received their glory, just as Miles

Davis, Elvis, and Whitney Houston did theirs; Woodrow Wilson, Ronald Reagan, and George H. W. Bush theirs also; Andrew Carnegie, David Rockefeller, and John McAfee theirs too. Their glory faded, because it did not consist in the honor that comes from God only. Unwisely, they sought a false glory rather than true glory, the latter glory which, as the Septuagint says, begins only with seeking God: "The fear of the Lord is honour, and glory, and gladness, and a crown of rejoicing" (Sir 1:11). For only the desire to know and love God brings glory, for it alone is destined to abide: "Therefore the desire of wisdom bringeth to the kingdom" (Wis 6:20).

Christ says, "I receive not honor from men" (John 5:41). Why does he not receive such honor? He receives their scorn rather than their praise, because "they have not the love of God" (John 5:42). Here we encounter perhaps the greatest of life's incomprehensibilities. Why, in short, do those who do not love God not love him? They love him not, you may say, because their deeds are evil. This is the explanation John records in that same Gospel account—namely, that those who do evil cannot face God but must turn away from him. But this simply pushes the question back, of course. For why, then, we might ask, are those who are evil that way? Why do they do what is evil? They do evil, you may say, because they are of their father, the devil (John 8:44). The devil himself is evil, and those who, like him, do not love God do as their father the devil does. If he is the first rebel, men who choose to be rebels themselves do as he has done. Yes, true enough, but this only pushes the question back still further. For even if we could explain the evil of men on account of diabolic influence, we would nevertheless be left to explain what accounts for the devil's own evil. Why did the devil choose to disobey God and rebel? Isaiah tells us quite rightly that it was pride, the desire to be as God (Isa 14:14). True enough, but this still does not explain why the devil formed this desire, much less why he chose to succumb to it. In the last analysis, evil is inscrutable. There is no making sense of it, because it simply makes no sense.[2]

2. This is Vladimir Jankélévitch's own compelling thesis. See Jankélévitch, *Forgiveness*, 57–156.

For this reason, those who work evil in life will be left speechless on the day of judgment. There will be no possibility of justifiably accounting for their deeds, for their deeds, which were evil, will be seen to be lacking any conceivable justification, for evil itself is the willing abandonment of all reason, and hence justification. Evil, in the last analysis, wills nothing but its own will, which is absurd. This is not to say, as many of the Greeks, such as Socrates, did, that nobody knowingly works evil.[3] It is quite possible to know something is evil and to do it anyway. Knowledge of the good does not suffice to ensure that one thereby will do it and abstain from what is not. Man is free, which means his desire always leaves it open for him to do what he knows to be evil. Working good or evil is not merely a rational exercise of the mind, it is an expression of the heart. To do what is evil, we see, ultimately is to desire not to be subject to God. It is to hate God rather than to love him. If we ask why, then, one would ever choose to be this way, we are left scratching our heads, for there is no reason, something that will be manifest on the last day, when those who chose to be so are left speechless, like the man who came to the king's wedding feast without any garment (Matt 21:11–13).[4]

To return to the subject of honor, we thus see why the praise of men must be hollow. The honor that comes from men is predicated on the world's glory, on the premise that deeds derive their significance and value in what men esteem. When acting for this esteem and praise of others, everything is done with an eye to witnesses. When acting with God, it is different. As Christ says, "I receive not testimony from men" (John 5:34). It is the Father

---

3. This Socratic intellectualism receives its strongest formulation in Plato's *Gorgias*. To maintain that such a view is mistaken and that human beings are indeed capable of knowingly doing wrong is not to deny that sin darkens the noetic faculties of the evildoer. An evil mind, to be sure, is a darkened one. But the fact remains that evil is always a choice, one rooted in the heart. No amount of knowledge can compel one to be good.

4. As Simone Weil says, evil deeds are done in darkness in that they are estranged from the good, which is why the one who does them cannot account for them: "When we do evil we do not know it, because evil flies from the light" (Weil, *Gravity and Grace*, 122).

who bears witness to him, though the world cannot see the Father. Christ's deeds, which are wrought in the Father, are not done in the light of the world, where men display themselves in order to garner praise and honor from others. Those who are of the world thus hate Christ, because he testifies that what they esteem so highly is not as great as they believe. All of their praise, esteem, and honor—this glory of the world—is a counterfeit glory.[5]

Like Christ, David also earned the scorn and ire of those he knew. As David says, "They have rewarded me evil for good, and hatred for my love" (Ps 108:5). Or again, as he says, "Those who render evil for good, they are my adversaries, because I follow what is good" (Ps 38:20). David, who was strong and wise and mighty among men, was viewed with scorn by these others. Despite all his greatness, he was hated rather than admired, as he rejected the world's glory. His glory was in the Lord. No matter what good you accomplish, the world will refuse to honor you if the good you have done was accomplished in God. Ultimately, the honor that comes from men is not predicated on esteeming greatness but is designed to silence God. This is precisely what Christ says: "You have not heard his voice at any time" (John 5:37), "you have not his word abiding in you" (John 5:38), and thus "I am come in my Father's name and you receive me not: if another shall come in his own name, him you will receive" (John 5:43). What prophetic, insightful words! Who will honestly deny them? How many thousands of men down through the centuries have come since Christ, men who have had their names received with gladness, men who have had their deeds extolled and who received so much honor?

5. Take the term "prestige," which in English is understood to signify someone or something possessing widespread respect or admiration. In French, however, *prestige* can connote trickery or illusion, in keeping with the Latin *praestigium*, itself signifying "delusion" or "illusion" (Etymonline, s.v. "prestige (n.)," https://www.etymonline.com/word/prestige). To say that the world's glory is counterfeit, thus, is to say its prestige is itself illusory, merely apparent. What the world takes to be riches are a case in point. The aim, for instance, of Christ's teaching to scorn pursuing wealth as an end in itself is meant to direct us to what really matters, to true glory. As the Septuagint says, "If riches be a possession to be desired in this life: what is richer than wisdom, that worketh all things?" (Wis 8:5).

You see, come in your own name as an actor, musician, tycoon, or politician and the world esteems you, the world admires you, the world honors you. Yes, then all the world's glory can be yours! But live in the name of Jesus Christ, he who himself was rejected for coming in his Father's name, and then you will be scorned too, for you have chosen to seek the honor that comes from God only. A beautiful actress, a gifted musician, a lucky tycoon, a mighty politician—the world can accept such types. The actress and musician entertain, the tycoon allures, the politician inspires. Of course, others partly resent that they are not themselves beautiful, alluring, lucky, or inspiring. But they can live with this—it does not ultimately dissuade them from heaping praise on those who are, because the actress, musician, tycoon, and politician have sought (and attained) the world's glory. Their successful lives provide an assurance that it is fine to do as they have done, to have sought the honor of men. And so, the world receives them! But seek the honor that comes from God only, and you also will be rejected just as David and Christ were; you, too, will be shown that your deeds, however great, are in the opinion of the world worthy of little more than its derision. For then your deeds bear witness of the Father, whom the world rejects. Those of the world can bear to be reminded that they are unsuccessful or unlucky in light of the world's glory, that they are not what it understands to be great— not an actor, musician, tycoon, or politician. But those of the world cannot bear to be reminded that the world's glory knows nothing of true greatness, that greatness really consists in winning the honor that comes from God only.

The actor is honored, because he is handsome and dashing, or at least likable. He is likable, because in his performance, he has let us feel something we perhaps have felt too, or wished we had felt. He is the rugged renegade, the daring criminal, the fearless hero, the dreamy lover. He takes us into an imaginary world that we ourselves think we wish were ours. We are timid and obsequious at the office, so we live vicariously through the iconoclast who comically disobeys his boss at work in ways we never would. We are too fearful ourselves to break the law and go to jail, so we live vicariously through the masked robber who holds up the bank and speeds away in the getaway car. We know of the world's corruption and injustice, but we say and do nothing about it, so we live vicariously through the caped hero who goes on a crusade against the city's villains. We are bored and dissatisfied with our partner, so we live vicariously through the seducer who makes adultery seem romantic. The actor, in providing us escape, allows us to feel as if we were better than we really are, to feel as if our life is more exciting than it really is. The actor makes others feel better about themselves and their lives by giving them a fantasy, and for this, the world repays him with its honor.

The musician is honored, because he is soulful and passionate, or at least endearing. He is endearing, because in his performance, he has let us feel something we perhaps have felt too, or wished we had felt. He gives voice to our pains and joys, our hopes and fears. He memorializes our rites of passage, our first kiss, our first date, our going away to college, our wedding day, our favorite vacation, our hope for some brighter tomorrow. We remember our youth, which is gone, but the musician in his song restores it. For a short moment, in listening, it is again as if present. We miss the past, which is gone, but the musician in his song revivifies it. We fear the future, which is uncertain, but the musician in his song consoles us with images of a desirable one to come. We feel alone, regretful over those we have hurt, pained by those who have hurt us, but the musician reconciles us as we listen, giving us comfort in knowing that these regrets and pains are not ours alone, but common to everyone. The musician makes others feel better about themselves and their lives by giving them an anesthetic, and for this, the world repays him with its honor.

The tycoon is honored, because he is crafty and domineering, or at least lucky. He is lucky, because in his display of exorbitant wealth, he has let us feel something we perhaps have felt too, or wished we had felt. He shows us what it is to actually have all we desire to possess for ourselves, all his money and power. He assures us that what motivates us to wake up and go to work every day is in fact worthwhile, that the money and success we dream of one day being ours as well is, if likely not attainable, still no less certainly admirable. In reading the newspapers headlines and watching the television interviews, we admire his luck and his fortune, and though we might blush to admit it to others, we secretly believe that we, too, might still one day be so lucky. Perhaps fortune will one day smile on us, as it already has on him. And if it does not, well, we can always take satisfaction in what we do have, knowing that it is possible to admire an enchanted world in which for some, if not us, dreams do come true, for fortune does indeed smile greatly on the few who are so lucky. The tycoon makes others feel better about themselves and their lives by giving them an idol, and for this, the world repays him with its honor.

The politician is honored, because he is charismatic and inspiring, or at least substantial. He is substantial, because in his speeches and debates, he has let us feel something we perhaps have felt too, or at least wished we had felt. He gives voice to our aspirations and idealizations, our dreams and visions. He is a figure of our own personalized conception of utopia, of the society we think would be best. In listening to him, we are reminded of what we think this world should be, maybe can be, which is why we admire all his fine words and serious demeanor. We know the world's corruption and injustice, and we might despair over its many problems. But not this man—no, not this politician! Yes, he still believes in progress. He says what we are too timid to say ourselves, too embarrassed to admit we still desire. He speaks candidly of hope and change, or of making things great again. He tells us what we wish we were able to tell others if we were on the stage. The politician makes others feel better about themselves and their lives by being their mouthpiece, and for this, the world repays him with its honor.

What, then, of Christ? Why does the world not honor him? It does not honor him, because he bears an entirely different form of witness. He does not speak of the world's glory; he does not speak of the importance and value of seeking the honor of men. He does not provide you with the assurance of the actor's fantasy, the musician's anesthetic, the tycoon's luck, or the politician's bullhorn.

To the contrary, he renounces all such glory and calls you to turn away from these illusions also. "Envy not the glory of a sinner, for thou knowest not what shall be his end" (Sir 9:11)—or rather, because the end of the sinner is a temporal and shallow glory, an apparent glory, pay it no mind and instead pursue eternal glory in Christ. Instead, he calls you back to yourself, to the same honor to which he bears witness, to the honor that comes from the Father only. Overturning the world's false glory, he reminds you that true greatness is to receive the world's scorn. For only the honor that comes from God alone is glorious.

Chapter 5

The Words I Have Spoken
to You Are Spirit

WHEN AT LAST THE heart awakens from its sleep, silencing the world's night, to see the light of Christ, it is not just the eyes that are illuminated. Its ears listen, and the heart hears the voice of Life, the Word who now is heard to speak to it. No longer does the heart discourse silently alone with itself. With the Word addressing it, what had been the heart's internal soliloquy is changed, now transformed into an incessant conversation with another. Henceforth, the words of life are ever present, resounding through the inner deep of the one they in turn guide. As the one born again comes thereby to realize, life now consists in walking with God.

The existence within the world oriented by God can itself be likened to comparatively mundane, perilous situations. When, for instance, on a narrow trail in a dark, thick wood, one looks straight above to the moon and stars, taking one step carefully at a time. When the power is out and the house is pitch dark, one reaches out to touch the wall, taking one step very carefully at a time. The world itself is a dark and obscure place, full of deceit and danger, a place where it is always possible to lose one's way.

But with Christ, the wood trail becomes traversable, for the light shines from above, illuminating the path to take. With Christ, the house without power becomes habitable, for the light shines like a candle, illuminating the room. When in the midst of a dark, thick wood at night, one would never dare shut one's eyes to the moon and stars, and when in a house without power, one would never put out one's candle. If to do so would be ludicrous, how much more ridiculous to attempt to navigate through the world without the light of Christ!

How grateful you would be for the moon above you in the thick wood, how thankful for the candle in your hand in the dark room, when the night would otherwise prevail over you, leaving you lost and alone. And yet, how much more grateful, how much more thankful, there is reason to be for the light of Christ, for the words we hear from him in our heart. This is what John's Gospel records. In the eighth chapter, Christ says, "I am the light of the world. He that follows me shall not walk in darkness, but shall have the light of life" (John 8:12). Where does this light shine but in the heart? As Christ says in that same chapter, "He that is of God hears God's words" (John 8:47). Shortly before his arrest in Gethsemane, Christ explains to his disciples the meaning of these words. It is the Spirit who will manifest himself to those who hear him, says Christ. Thus, in response to a disciple who has just asked how God will make himself manifest, yet at the same time not manifest to the world, Christ responds by saying, "If a man love me, he will keep my words, and my Father will love him, and we will come unto him, and make our abode in him" (John 14:23). That Christ is speaking here of the Spirit becomes even more apparent in the very next chapter, when he says plainly, "But when the Comforter is come, whom I will send unto you from the Father, even the Spirit of truth, which proceeds from the Father, he shall testify of me" (John 15:26). What a wondrous marvel! In listening to the Word, the heart that has opened itself to these words the world cannot hear receives a reply in the form of the Spirit, who speaks. The words of Christ, the words of life, reverberate in the heart of the one attuned to them.

ength would have been insufficient to carry on.
gives us wings.
rom God when there is no help from elsewhere.
ch circumstances powerfully when relating his
ecutions at the hands of enemies. The light of
never abandons us. This is not always the case
ourse. As David himself discovers, in the midst
s, very often we find ourselves alone, abandoned
ht have expected to be there for us. He laments
ing, "Thou has put far from me every friend" (Ps
imes of separation, we may well feel alone. To be
e, inasmuch as others fail to come to one's aid.
re are instead only the constant attacks: "Keep me
which they have set for me, and from stumbling-
that work iniquity. Sinners shall fall by their own
until I escape" (Ps 140:9-10). "There was none that
oul," says David during this period of isolation. "I
ry low; deliver me from them that persecute me;
onger than I. Bring my soul out of prison, that I
ks to thy name, O Lord" (Ps 141:4-7). Like Job, the
oppression take their toll, as David says: "I am worn
y enemies" (Ps 6:7). But as David recounts, without
m we can turn, we learn that it was always God who
ted. Having forgotten God during the easy times, we
of his steadfastness during the hard times, since he
e there for us in our distress when others have fled.
The Lord preserves the souls of his saints; he shall
from the hand of sinners. Light is sprung up for the
d gladness for the upright in heart" (Ps 96:10-12).
eatest periods of darkness, when we are most isolated
n by others, God reveals that he has never abandoned
we must consequently learn to depend on him, since
es us as nobody else does.
otion of our dependence on divine love and the way in
engthens us receives its most beautiful—and famous—
n in the words of Isaiah. He writes, "But those who wait

Aside from being applicable words, words we may live by, they are precious words for that very reason. They are words that provide light, that render a situation intelligible that would otherwise not be so. Without the moon and stars in the wood above, without the candle in the room, darkness would overtake us. The moon and the candle give us the one thing needful: light. But the light of Christ is even more precious. For not only is it a needful light, one without which we would be lost, it is a light that speaks to us. It speaks, because it is a light that knows the darkness from which it keeps us. For all its beauty, the moon's pallid light does not know the fear and danger of being lost in the dark wood below. For all its comfort, the candle's warm flame does not know the disorientation of stumbling through the dark room. The moon and the candle dispel the night's darkness, but they themselves know nothing of it. With the light of Christ, it is different. For the light of Christ proves itself capable of revealing the way to us only because Christ himself knows the very darkness with which he helps us contend. The light of Christ is capable of overcoming the world's darkness, as he himself was acquainted with it as a man also. He has known the danger, known the darkness of temptation and evil. He has seen and experienced human suffering and sorrow. He has undergone the cruelty and mockery of others. He has been persecuted and hated. In short, he knows what it is like to find oneself surrounded by darkness, abandoned by everyone, left for nothing, as if he were a nobody deserving of such treatment. The candle or the moon does not know that others need them. But Christ does. And for this reason, he can speak of this gracious light that overcomes the darkness, for he knows the Father of Lights, the one to whom he bore witness during his life as a man on the earth. Moonlight and candlelight are precious things, to be sure. But how much more precious this light of Christ, this light that overcomes darkness, because it has experienced the same darkness from which it delivers us.

The room without the candle's flame, the wood trail without the moon—these are great darknesses. The heart without the light of the Word shining within it, however, is a much greater darkness.

For this reason, the Bible itself equates the heart that has been illuminated by Christ as a lamp whose light has been lit but had once been darkness. This is a recurring theme in the Psalms of David, for instance. David says, "For you will light my lamp; the Lord my God will enlighten my darkness" (Ps 17:28). And again, "Your word is a lamp to my feet, and a light to my path" (Ps 119:105). David accentuates the uniqueness of this light. Like other lights, it illuminates what previously was shrouded in darkness. And that is important. But there is more. For unlike the light of the moon, which is capable of guiding us from above, or the candle flame which we hold out before us, the light of Christ is with us by walking with us. Taking us by the hand—that is to say, by the hands of the heart—these words of life point out the way and order the heart's footsteps to take. The Word, residing within the heart, illuminates the path forward: it is a lamp to the heart's feet. Listening to the Word, thus, is hearing wisdom. Following the dictates of wisdom, then, as the Septuagint relates, ensures that "if he do them, he shall be strong to all things: for the light of the Lord is his path" (Sir 50:29). This is why, in the Proverbs also, the importance of following this light is emphasized. To follow the light of Christ is to trust what it has revealed, to take the path it has illumined. As it says, "Trust in the Lord with all your heart, and be not exalted in your own wisdom. In all your ways acquaint thyself with her, that she might rightly direct your paths" (Prov 3:5-6). This, then, is the light of life, the light of the Word, which, illuminating the heart, at once guides and directs the one whose lamp has been lit by it. Hence, as Christ accordingly says, such is the one who shall not stumble in darkness.

But this light—the light of the Spirit, this light which is unlike any other light, unlike the moon or the candle—is even more versatile than this. For in addition to lighting the lamp of our heart, thereby directing our path through the dangers of the world's darkness, this same light can equally, when necessary, serve as a stronghold or a shield. This is why David will sometimes compare the light of God to a high tower. David says, "The Lord is my light and my salvation, whom shall I fear? The Lord is the strength

of my life, of whor
my enemies and my
stumbled and fell" (
for the one in whom
yet cannot penetrate
stumble and fall, for l
selves in darkness, inc
poses them. As David
and my deliverer; my (
buckler, and the horn (
call upon the Lord, who
from mine enemies" (Ps
says, "When my heart is
is higher than I. For thou
tower from the enemy. I
will trust in the cover of tl
of the light of God to a h
of course. As the Proverbs
tower. The righteous run to

This light is more vers
the lamp of one's heart, a li
path, neither is it only a forti
tion. Additionally, it strength
farther than would be possible
sustains. As David says, "Be of
strengthened" (Ps 30:24). In th
Psalms, David likens such light
if the Proverbs identify the "nan
this name, we know, is the Wo
light of Christ, and thus in his w(
Such light renews the strength o
reached the limits of his own po
then, only illuminate a path forw
upon it. Nor does it even simply a
us. Moreover, and essentially, it ca

when our own str
The light of Christ
Help comes f
David recounts su
own various pers
God, as he says,
with others, of c
of our worst trial
by those we mig
the isolation, say
87:18). In such t
sure, one *is* alor
From others, the
from the snare
blocks of them
net: I am alone
cared for my s
am brought ve
for they are st
may give than
isolation and c
out from all m
others to who
was to be trus
are reminded
is the only or
David says,
deliver them
righteous, a
Amid our g
and forgotte
us and that
he alone lov
This n
which it str
formulatio

on the Lord shall renew their strength. They shall mount up with wings like eagles. They shall run and not be weary. They shall walk and not faint" (Isa 40:31). What precious light! A light not only lighting our path forward but accompanying us along it, providing us a fortress when we need refuge, even giving us wings when our feet would otherwise give out. Here, perhaps, it is fitting to close by mentioning just one more related figure this light is said to take. For very often, we find it equated with breath. As Job says, "But it is a spirit in man, and the breath of the Almighty gives them understanding" (Job 32:8). As already mentioned, this is what John learned as well from Christ. It is the breath of God, the Holy Spirit, who shines his light, dispelling all darkness, all confusion. As Christ says, "But the Comforter, the Holy Spirit, whom the Father will send in My name, he will teach you all things, and bring to your remembrance all that I said to you" (John 14:26). The same lesson is repeated again just two chapters later in John's Gospel, where Christ says, "But when he, the Spirit of truth, comes, he will guide you into all the truth" (John 16:13). In Greek, after all, the word for Spirit, *pneuma* (πνεῦμα), also signifies breath. This, hence, is the light that gives breath, the power of the Holy Spirit, who bestows understanding and strength on the one in whose heart he dwells.

Such is the light of life of which Christ speaks, the Spirit of truth—this light which overcomes the world, so that we might not stumble amid the darkness. Accordingly, only one question becomes essential: Do you yourself yet have this breath—have you yet heard these words, these words the Word has spoken to you?

Chapter 6

The Worries of This Life

JOHN THE BAPTIST, WHO was a messenger from the Lord, understood quite well our basic and ultimate dependence on God.[1] His utterances give it constant expression. For example, in answer to his critics questioning his authority to speak for the Lord, he says, "A man can receive nothing, except it be given him from heaven" (John 3:27). Everything, even our very breath, as the Baptist says, is a gift from above, something for which we ourselves are not the origin. Our lives themselves can be likened to a series of fleeting breaths, because the breath of life sustaining them in being at any moment can be withdrawn, as eventually it will be. This theme of breath is not only pertinent to John the Baptist's message of dependence, then. David's words are words of dependence also: "Man is like a breath. His days are like a passing shadow" (Ps 144:4 KJV). What dependence! That the breath itself we breathe is not ours— that the force of life enlivening us is something we are unable to give to ourselves and maintain but must receive, must receive from

1. Here, naturally, one calls to mind Friedrich Schleiermacher's thesis, according to which the essence of Christian faith is said to reside in the "the feeling of absolute dependence on God," or perhaps the "absolute feeling of dependence on God." For more on the matter, see Behrens, "Feeling of Absolute Dependence," 471–81.

the Spirit, the breath of God. It is this absolute dependence upon God which Christ himself attempts to remind us of when, in Mark's Gospel, he speaks of the vital importance of listening to God, of hearing what God says to us through the Spirit. As Christ says, "If any man has ears to hear, let him hear" (Mark 4:23). For any living man who takes the time seriously to ponder what it means to be alive—to be a living being imbued from elsewhere with the breath of life, a breath he is powerless to give to himself—let him, then, hear what this breath of life, the Word, has to say about life. What do we hear if we listen?

To begin with, any life led without an acknowledgment of its dependence on the breath of God eventually only suffocates itself. Let us illustrate with an example. Someone who is drowning in the sea close to shore finds himself choking on the water. In a panic, this swimmer thrashes violently, trying desperately to cling to the life he feels escaping. And yet, by fighting so furiously to clear his throat and keep his head above water, by attempting to draw breath as he does, he only worsens the situation and, ultimately, drowns. In just this way, the passion of unruly desires can be likened to this swimmer. You see, man was born on the shores of grace, on the firm land of God. "And the Lord God formed man of the dust of the ground, and breathed into his nostrils the breath of life; and man became a living being" (Gen 2:7). But in life, there comes a time in which we forget this, and, as we leave our natural station, desire leads us out into the world, which itself can be likened to a perilous sea. This is where our swimmer finds himself, and why he drowns. For the more he thrashed in the water, the more it simply flooded him, until finally there was no breath of life at all. He died at sea, with the land all the while still in sight. Such a drowning proved to be a self-induced choking. How better it would have been for the swimmer who began drowning to have taken a deep breath and paused, to have stopped violently thrashing, and to have calmly awaited rescue from shore, to have awaited the lifeboat or the lifeguard. Perhaps he could have even attempted to swim to land rather than thrash in the same place. But the drowning victim who succumbed to the water in the way we've just described would not do so. His desire became a vortex, something whose undertow is far stronger than any ocean's riptide. Overtaken by panic and confusion, the drowning swimmer fought to the very end, to be sure, but this fighting was entirely foolish, for, unable to sustain himself against the tides, he inevitably succumbed to the water. We might imagine the lifeguard retrieving his lifeless body from the water and laying it out on the shore. The lifeguard attempts to restore the breath of life back into his lungs, but it is of no avail. Now it is too late, for the breath of life has permanently withdrawn, and he is expired. The crowd of onlookers who are assembled around the lifeguard might find this particular drowning especially tragic, as it was so senseless. For ironically, the swimmer constricted his own breathing by having strained so hard to take control over it.

How avoidable it all was! To continue with our analogy, liken the sea to the world and the beach shore to grace. Christ is the lifeguard there to oversee things. He has warned you and everyone there of the conditions and has told you all to take caution. Before our swimmer took the plunge, he had seen the waves and knew of the danger. He was warned of the riptides and had seen other swimmers struggle out to sea, only barely to return to shore alive. But he did not listen. He disregarded the many signs of danger and, assured of himself and his own capacities, went out to swim alone, confident that he would be fine. When the trouble befell him, he would not admit to himself the true danger he was in, and so rather than coming to shore when he still could, he remained out in the water, until finally it overtook him and he went under. This swimmer made his decision and faced the consequences. But for the others who have seen what came of him, there is still hope. Hope that they will not do the same. Now, then, liken Christ to the lifeguard and everyone in the world to these other swimmers who still have a choice. What does Christ tell these swimmers? He tells them clearly, "Come unto me, all ye that labour and are heavy laden, and I will give you rest" (Matt 11:28). You see, when a swimmer drowns in the sea, the others who have been lucky enough not to be him recognize the danger and come to shore, lest they suffer the same fate. But this is where the analogy admittedly fails. For in

Aside from being applicable words, words we may live by, they are precious words for that very reason. They are words that provide light, that render a situation intelligible that would otherwise not be so. Without the moon and stars in the wood above, without the candle in the room, darkness would overtake us. The moon and the candle give us the one thing needful: light. But the light of Christ is even more precious. For not only is it a needful light, one without which we would be lost, it is a light that speaks to us. It speaks, because it is a light that knows the darkness from which it keeps us. For all its beauty, the moon's pallid light does not know the fear and danger of being lost in the dark wood below. For all its comfort, the candle's warm flame does not know the disorientation of stumbling through the dark room. The moon and the candle dispel the night's darkness, but they themselves know nothing of it. With the light of Christ, it is different. For the light of Christ proves itself capable of revealing the way to us only because Christ himself knows the very darkness with which he helps us contend. The light of Christ is capable of overcoming the world's darkness, as he himself was acquainted with it as a man also. He has known the danger, known the darkness of temptation and evil. He has seen and experienced human suffering and sorrow. He has undergone the cruelty and mockery of others. He has been persecuted and hated. In short, he knows what it is like to find oneself surrounded by darkness, abandoned by everyone, left for nothing, as if he were a nobody deserving of such treatment. The candle or the moon does not know that others need them. But Christ does. And for this reason, he can speak of this gracious light that overcomes the darkness, for he knows the Father of Lights, the one to whom he bore witness during his life as a man on the earth. Moonlight and candlelight are precious things, to be sure. But how much more precious this light of Christ, this light that overcomes darkness, because it has experienced the same darkness from which it delivers us.

The room without the candle's flame, the wood trail without the moon—these are great darknesses. The heart without the light of the Word shining within it, however, is a much greater darkness.

For this reason, the Bible itself equates the heart that has been illuminated by Christ as a lamp whose light has been lit but had once been darkness. This is a recurring theme in the Psalms of David, for instance. David says, "For you will light my lamp; the Lord my God will enlighten my darkness" (Ps 17:28). And again, "Your word is a lamp to my feet, and a light to my path" (Ps 119:105). David accentuates the uniqueness of this light. Like other lights, it illuminates what previously was shrouded in darkness. And that is important. But there is more. For unlike the light of the moon, which is capable of guiding us from above, or the candle flame which we hold out before us, the light of Christ is with us by walking with us. Taking us by the hand—that is to say, by the hands of the heart—these words of life point out the way and order the heart's footsteps to take. The Word, residing within the heart, illuminates the path forward: it is a lamp to the heart's feet. Listening to the Word, thus, is hearing wisdom. Following the dictates of wisdom, then, as the Septuagint relates, ensures that "if he do them, he shall be strong to all things: for the light of the Lord is his path" (Sir 50:29). This is why, in the Proverbs also, the importance of following this light is emphasized. To follow the light of Christ is to trust what it has revealed, to take the path it has illumined. As it says, "Trust in the Lord with all your heart, and be not exalted in your own wisdom. In all your ways acquaint thyself with her, that she might rightly direct your paths" (Prov 3:5–6). This, then, is the light of life, the light of the Word, which, illuminating the heart, at once guides and directs the one whose lamp has been lit by it. Hence, as Christ accordingly says, such is the one who shall not stumble in darkness.

But this light—the light of the Spirit, this light which is unlike any other light, unlike the moon or the candle—is even more versatile than this. For in addition to lighting the lamp of our heart, thereby directing our path through the dangers of the world's darkness, this same light can equally, when necessary, serve as a stronghold or a shield. This is why David will sometimes compare the light of God to a high tower. David says, "The Lord is my light and my salvation, whom shall I fear? The Lord is the strength

of my life, of whom should I be afraid? When the wicked, even
my enemies and my foes, came upon me to eat up my flesh, they
stumbled and fell" (Ps 26:1–2). Here the light of God is a refuge
for the one in whom it resides, a fortress the wicked can storm
yet cannot penetrate. Indeed, as David says, those who attack it
stumble and fall, for lacking the light they attack, they find themselves in darkness, incapable of prevailing against the light that op-
poses them. As David says, "The Lord is my rock, and my fortress,
and my deliverer; my God, my strength, in whom I will trust; my
buckler, and the horn of my salvation, and my high tower. I will
call upon the Lord, who is worthy to be praised: so shall I be saved
from mine enemies" (Ps 18:2–3 KJV). Or, as the King James again
says, "When my heart is overwhelmed, lead me to the rock that
is higher than I. For thou hast been a shelter for me, and a strong
tower from the enemy. I will abide in thy tabernacle for ever. I
will trust in the cover of thy wings" (Ps 61:2–3 KJV). The equation
of the light of God to a high tower is not limited to the Psalms,
of course. As the Proverbs say, "The name of the Lord is a strong
tower. The righteous run to it and are safe" (Prov 18:10 LXX).

This light is more versatile still. Aside from being a light to
the lamp of one's heart, a light in turn capable of directing one's
path, neither is it only a fortress providing a refuge from persecution. Additionally, it strengthens the one in whom it shines to go
farther than would be possible without it. In a word, it is a light that
sustains. As David says, "Be of good courage, and let your heart be
strengthened" (Ps 30:24). In the passage cited previously from the
Psalms, David likens such light to something having "wings." And
if the Proverbs identify the "name of the Lord" with a strong tower,
this name, we know, is the Word. Those who seek refuge in the
light of Christ, and thus in his words, find comfort and protection.
Such light renews the strength of whoever would otherwise have
reached the limits of his own power. The light of God does not,
then, only illuminate a path forward, helping us orient ourselves
upon it. Nor does it even simply assist us by walking along it with
us. Moreover, and essentially, it carries us forward, propelling us

Faint Not

when our own strength would have been insufficient to carry on. The light of Christ gives us wings.

Help comes from God when there is no help from elsewhere. David recounts such circumstances powerfully when relating his own various persecutions at the hands of enemies. The light of God, as he says, never abandons us. This is not always the case with others, of course. As David himself discovers, in the midst of our worst trials, very often we find ourselves alone, abandoned by those we might have expected to be there for us. He laments the isolation, saying, "Thou has put far from me every friend" (Ps 87:18). In such times of separation, we may well feel alone. To be sure, one *is* alone, inasmuch as others fail to come to one's aid. From others, there are instead only the constant attacks: "Keep me from the snare which they have set for me, and from stumbling-blocks of them that work iniquity. Sinners shall fall by their own net: I am alone until I escape" (Ps 140:9–10). "There was none that cared for my soul," says David during this period of isolation. "I am brought very low; deliver me from them that persecute me; for they are stronger than I. Bring my soul out of prison, that I may give thanks to thy name, O Lord" (Ps 141:4–7). Like Job, the isolation and oppression take their toll, as David says: "I am worn out from all my enemies" (Ps 6:7). But as David recounts, without others to whom we can turn, we learn that it was always God who was to be trusted. Having forgotten God during the easy times, we are reminded of his steadfastness during the hard times, since he is the only one there for us in our distress when others have fled. David says, "The Lord preserves the souls of his saints; he shall deliver them from the hand of sinners. Light is sprung up for the righteous, and gladness for the upright in heart" (Ps 96:10–12). Amid our greatest periods of darkness, when we are most isolated and forgotten by others, God reveals that he has never abandoned us and that we must consequently learn to depend on him, since he alone loves us as nobody else does.

This notion of our dependence on divine love and the way in which it strengthens us receives its most beautiful—and famous—formulation in the words of Isaiah. He writes, "But those who wait

50

the world, so very few ever come to Christ for rest. They struggle alone, scorning the shore, refusing to accept the limits of their own strength. Why do those exhausting themselves in the world, those still able to make it back to the shores of grace, persist in their futile struggle, fighting ferociously against the water, by ignoring God's warning to come to land?

They do not hear. But why do they not hear? They do not hear, because they do not listen, as they already are in a state of frenzy. Christ asks them whether they hear what God is saying—that they must come to shore right now—but they ignore this question and keep thrashing. Like the swimmer who has just drowned before them, they continue flailing. Overcome by their passions, they are oblivious to the lurking riptide ready to sweep them under. In short, the Word, which is the breath of life, has been choked. They have chocked the breath of life by thinking they are the masters of their own breath. As Christ says, "And the cares of this world, and the deceitfulness of riches, and the lusts of other things entering in, choke the word, and it becometh unfruitful" (Mark 4:19). Although the metaphor Christ employs to explain the danger of failing to depend on God is not aquatic, the point stands. To choke the word is to choke away the breath of life by relying solely on oneself, rather than the Spirit, to provide that breath.

These lusts from which Christ attempts to dissuade us are like the seawater that fills up the lungs. For just as the sea's raging waters fill up our lungs until we can no longer breath, so too lust fills up the heart with a torrent choking out the word of God. If the Word is ever to breathe freely within us, the heart must be made empty to receive it, certainly not full of lust. But the Bible extends this analogy between lust and breath further. For not only do vain lusts choke out the word of God, such that God cannot dwell in us, these lusts can be likened to a great wind that takes us off course, directing us to destruction. A lust that fails to satisfy is a failed lust. Yet, this is what such lusts lead to inevitably—to frustration, disappointment, emptiness. As James says in his letter, "You lust, and have not" (Jas 4:2). Or again, "You ask, and receive not, because you ask amiss, that you may consume it upon your lusts" (Jas 4:3). As Isaiah puts it, "'There is no peace,' says the Lord, 'for the wicked'" (Isa 48:22). There is no rest, because there is only lust, and so there is no satisfaction. There is no need to repeat again the preceding analyses regarding this despair of time that knows nothing besides these vain desires. As we have seen, they accomplish nothing but the desire for more, a desire that proves unquenchable, because it never finds any satisfaction even in what it attains. What is interesting is how James compares this life of vain desire, of lust, to a breeze that does not accept its own fleetingness. He describes the mentality of those who are subject to their lusts thusly: "Today or tomorrow we will go into such a city, and continue there a year, and buy and sell, and get gain. Whereas ye know not what shall be on the morrow. For what is your life? It is even a vapor, that appears for a little time, and then vanishes away" (Jas 4:13–14). Such a life knows nothing yet of gratitude, for it fails to acknowledge that its very life, which in its brevity is equated to a vapor, depends on the breath of God, the very breath upon which it refuses to depend. As James says, "'For you ought to say, If the Lord will, we shall live, and do this, or that. But now you rejoice in your boastings; all such rejoicing is evil'" (Jas 4:15–16).

When, then, you have so choked the word of God out of you, so that now there is no room for it in your heart—for your lusts and desires have rendered you unfeeling to anything else but themselves—only an emergency stands any chance of alerting you to the danger of which you have become unaware. Suppose you are the one drowning. When drowning in the sea, if you keep your wits, you will look to the shore for any sign of a helping hand. And when drowning amid the world's lusts, where else will this hand come but from God? Isaiah, for this reason, equates the grace that God extends us to a hand. He says, "For I the Lord thy God will hold thy right hand, saying unto thee, Fear not; I will help thee" (Isa 41:13). For just as the Bible draws a parallel between lust and breath—or rather, how lust suffocates the breath of God—so too it equates the dangers of the world, particularly evil and death, as a flood, one capable of drowning us. As David says, "The sorrows of death compassed me, and the floods of ungodly men made me afraid" (Ps 18:4). Or again, as David says, "Let me not sink, let me be delivered from them that hate me, and out of the deep waters. Let not the waterflood overflow me, neither let the deep swallow me up, and let not the pit shut her mouth upon me" (Ps 68:14–15). If you were drowning in the waves and glanced back to shore, imagine your despair if the lifeguard were merely to stare blankly at you and leave you to yourself. Perhaps you could accept that the others who are safe on the beach don't care. Perhaps they are too occupied with the joys before them—feeding the gulls, flying a kite, eating a picnic, or enjoying the view. In your distress, you might resent them for not noticing you. But the lifeguard! No, if the lifeguard were to look coldly upon you from his tower, only to then look away, your heart would sink even before the water could fill up your lungs. Just imagine, in fact, if the lifeguard were not only to look indifferently on you but to smirk, to wave at you mockingly, to actively delight in your plight. You might think you deserve to be drowning as you are, for you ignored the lifeguard, but you might rightly think that there is no justification for the lifeguard to mock you, to abandon you. After all, is it not the life-guard's duty to show you mercy, to save you, even when you are in need of saving only because of your own ignorance and foolish-ness? Yes, just imagine that the lifeguard sat idly at his tower while other swimmers were attempting to take you under and drown you! If we think no human lifeguard should ever allow such things, how much more so of God? Thankfully, God has more patience and mercy than any human lifeguard. He knows human frailty and pride, even if he doesn't approve it. His mercy is greater than our stupidity. And so, when we are in danger, even if it is ultimately self-induced, there is always the possibility of looking to God for rescue.

This is what the apostles learn for themselves in a situation, like the one described above, that happens to be aquatic. They are at sea in a frail boat. It is night, the waves are furious, and the winds are howling. They are in great jeopardy of being thrown into the sea, where they believe they will surely be drowned. Mark recounts the episode as follows: "Jesus was in the stern, asleep on a pillow. And they awoke him and said to him, 'Teacher, do you not care that we are perishing?' Then he arose and rebuked the wind, and said to the sea, 'Peace, be still!' And the wind ceased and there was a great calm. But he said to them, 'Why are you so fearful? How is it that you have no faith?'" (Mark 4:38–40). What to them appeared to be a great storm was in fact a mild tempest. For the power of God far exceeds any of the natural events over which he stands. As man, Christ demonstrates faith in this power by sleeping contentedly when the others are in a panic. As God, he demonstrates this power by showing them he possesses dominion over his creation. The storm is quickly calmed, the boat does not capsize, they do not drown, and the apostles are admonished for their lack of faith. The apostles, in a way, were in a far more enviable position when compared to whoever is still out swimming alone. For at least they were already with Christ, for they thought they understood the safety he provided. For them, Christ was serving as the ark of their life, the vessel there to protect them from the world's floods of ungodliness and evil. They, at least, were already in the boat with Christ. And when apparent danger struck, they, moreover, knew to look to Christ to save them. True enough, they exhibited fear where they shouldn't have. This evident momentary lapse of faith notwithstanding, even their fear still presupposed a recognition of their ultimate dependence on God. For when they were in distress, they immediately looked to the Word as the absolute horizon of all human experience. They did not look to the boat itself for safety but to him.

This, thus, is life's merciful ark, the merciful lifeguard always watching from the shores of grace, always willing to help the swimmers drowning in the world's flood of evil and despair. This is the one who, as the Word of Life, remains present even when we fear we are about to be drowned in some self-induced plight, and who offers to rescue us from ourselves anyway. This is the breath of life that is always there to breathe life back into us, if only we are first willing to empty ourselves of our own breath of pride and, no longer choking the Word with our worries and wayward desires, allow him to breathe within us.

Part 2

Chapter 7

For All That Is in the World

HAS CHRIST YET RESCUED you? Do you yourself now know God's salvation—this salvation, this new life—that frees anyone who has received it from evil and death? How magnificent a salvation! If you know this love of God that has delivered you from evil, then you will know why Thomas, who followed Christ, could look death in the face and say so calmly, "Let us also go, that we may die with him" (John 11:16). Yes, for how magnificent is this salvation that, delivering us from sin, the flesh, and the devil, renders even death itself nothing, along with all else that is in the world. Do you yet know this love the world does not know? If you still don't, then let us nevertheless try to reveal, as best as possible, what lies awaiting you along this path to eternal life should you ever choose to embark upon it. Only the joy of the Lord, you will see, will be capable of ensuring that those who take this path faint not but endure in the face of all that is in the world. For the world hates God, and so too it thus hates anyone who, loving him, strives to be with him forever in the kingdom of heaven. As Christ says unequivocally, "You shall be hated of all men for my name's sake, but he that endures to the end shall be saved" (Matt 10:22). What explains this hate?

Such hatred, in part, is rooted in the unwillingness to be reminded that what those of the world love—namely, all that is in the world—is opposed to the love of God. By loving what they do, they make themselves enemies of God. The fact that their love of all that is in the world is ultimately equivalent to a hatred of God can largely be suppressed in daily life, so long as they are surrounded only by other worldly people who share their desires and values, who are themselves men of the world, immersed in the worries of life, oblivious to eternity and the promise of eternal life. But place a follower of Christ in such people's midst, and the light of truth shines, a light those still existing in darkness cannot bear to face. They do not want to be reminded of death, much less of their accountability to God. From their perspective, the lover of God is an intruder and a traitor, someone who has forsaken all that is in the world for a kingdom that is not of this world. For not only does the lover of God hold all that is in the world with contempt, but the lover of God, simply by living as he does, reminds others that they, too, will ultimately be judged by God. This is what those living to enjoy themselves in the world cannot stand to be reminded of—that God will hold them accountable for this choice. For it is a choice! It is only revealed to be a choice, however, when the lover of God intrudes, for while in the presence of worldly others, it is possible for those who love the world to pretend that they do not hate God. In short, the lover of God is an offense to those who love all that is in the world, for the lover of God is a reminder of the very God who they themselves have rejected and attempted to forget. To encounter the lover of God, thus, is to experience a micro-eschaton,[1] a tiny foretaste of the final judgment. When, then, Christ tells his followers that if others will hate them, they have hated him first, this is because the follower of Christ reminds these others of him.

Two passages from Paul's letters—one to the Romans, the other to Timothy—illustrate well what becomes of those who, suppressing the truth of God, live solely for whatever they take to be

1. Jean-Yves Lacoste has discussed this notion of a *micro-eschatologie*, albeit in a different context. See Lacoste, *Être en danger*, 265–88.

gain in this world. Paul defines the reprobate mind as that which doesn't want to retain knowledge of God, that which wants to forget God. The result is an orgy of lust. As he details, such people become "filled with all unrighteousness, fornication, wickedness, covetousness, maliciousness; full of envy, murder, debate, deceit, malignity; whisperers, backbiters, haters of God, despiteful, proud, boasters, inventors of evil things, disobedient to parents, without understanding, covenant-breakers, without natural affection, implacable, unmerciful. Who knowing the judgment of God, that they which commit such things are worthy of death, not only do the same, but have pleasure in them that do them" (Rom 1:29–32). When discussing what he terms the "last days," Paul again lays out stridently what will become of those who do not strive to inherit the promise of eternal life but instead choose to live comfortably for all that is in the world. He says, "This know also, that in the last days perilous times shall come. For men shall be lovers of their own selves, covetous, boasters, proud, blasphemers, disobedient to parents, unthankful, unholy, without natural affection, truce-breakers, false accusers, incontinent, fierce, despisers of those that are good, traitors, heady, high-minded, lovers of pleasures more than lovers of God. Having a form of godliness, but denying the power thereof: from such turn away. For of this sort are they which creep into houses, and lead captive silly women laden with sins, led away with divers lusts, ever learning, and never able to come to the knowledge of the truth" (2 Tim 3:7).

But this is much too harsh, you will say! You know many, many people who do not yet know God yet who are, well, if not quite holy people, certainly not so evil as Paul has just described them. In daily life, after all, we frequently call such people—those who are rather nondescript, neither overtly holy or wicked—"good people." What does the world see in the figure of this "good person"?

Let us take an example. You are at a party. It is your wife's holiday work party. You don't want to go, but you go anyway. At the party, everyone is wearing an ugly sweater. There are drinks and snacks. The boss makes a speech, congratulating everyone on their year's fine work. He is proud of them. They are a team, even a family. As you listen to the speech, you look around the room. Your wife's coworkers, you see, know the boss is lying. He does not truly care about any of his workers here in the room. They are useful to him, and so long as they remain useful, he will keep them around. But if they cease being useful, they will be fired and the office will move on, as if the worker in question never existed. This is anything but a family, and it is frankly preposterous that the boss should say that it is. But this is the world! And so, great swelling words of emptiness as these are allowed, even expected. The workers listen quietly, nodding their heads approvingly, forcing a smile, and sipping their champagne. They have to be here; they don't want to be fired, for they need the money. If the boss wants to insult their intelligence by pretending that they all have something together everyone knows they really don't, well, so be it. When the speech concludes, everyone goes about mingling. There are introductions as the spouses of each worker meet the others from the office. People state their names, shake hands, and say a little bit about themselves. Those with children compare notes—where their children go to school, what their hobbies are, vacation spots they're planning to visit. They forge a fleeting, superficial bond in light of whatever commonality might happen to unite them. When you are there, you meet a husband from your same home state, or you meet a wife who roots for the same baseball team as your college best friend, etc., etc. When the party begins to wind down, it's time to leave. You get into the car, and your wife asks you about one of the people you met that night.

"What do you think about Claire?" your wife asks.

"I don't know. I guess she seems like a good person," you might say.

Ah! But what does this mean? You spoke to Claire for a handful of minutes—spoke to her about the most everyday, trivial of things. You do not really know Claire. You know nothing about her past. You certainly know nothing substantial about her heart. True enough, she was relatively pleasant, someone with whom you were able to maintain a brief conversation with ease. But does this qualify for making her, or anyone, a "good person"? How strange that in the world we so habitually apply the notion of good to someone we hardly know, someone who for all we know is far from good at all! Perhaps, unbeknownst to you, Claire is having an affair with the boss, who is married and whose wife was right there at the party listening to the speech about teamwork and family. Or perhaps Claire abuses her children at home. Or perhaps Claire is a thief who steals from the clothing stores she shops at. Or perhaps Claire hates your own wife and is secretly spreading nasty slanders about her around the office in a plot to steal your wife's job. If Claire succeeds, you and your wife won't be at next year's holiday party, and nobody who is still there will care or say a word. Yes, for all you really know, Claire is far from being a good person, and yet we all say so: she is a "good person"! The point of the illustration isn't to recommend suspicion or cynicism. Of course, we shouldn't conclude someone is wicked without having evidence, but at the same time, how superficial and foolish to so cavalierly declare that someone whom we hardly know at all is a "good person," simply because we've had a very brief interaction at a holiday work party. If nothing else, you see, the world's conception of goodness is remarkably shallow. How many years did John Wayne Gacy or Jeffrey Dahmer pass themselves off in the world as a "good person"? It says something about the world's superficiality and exceedingly low threshold for virtue that some of the evilest men to ever walk the earth were for a long time considered "good people"—ordinary neighbors, coworkers, and friends. You see, in the world, it takes precious little to have others say you are a "good person." Almost without exception, everyone is!

But what does the Bible say about goodness? Does it treat goodness so cheaply? Far from it, of course! Goodness is something precious and accordingly rare. The world's illusion of goodness as common and unremarkable is precisely what the law of God dispels. Nearly anyone can pass himself off to others as a good person when considered from the perspective of the world. But is one a good person when measured by God? That is the question! And as it happens, this is the very question that so many of the good people in the world hate to ask themselves. What happens when these good people are confronted with the law of God? Those who do not love God but were thought to be good people nonetheless, transform. Beneath the affability and kindness lies a fury. Here, it is necessary to correct another misconception about goodness, one enshrined by a popular theological myth. According to this view, which simply reverses the world's illusion of goodness as the norm, everyone is said to be irrevocably wicked and evil. Augustine, however, who introduced this notion, one in turn codified by Luther and Calvin, was entirely wrong in asserting that man is born depraved. Man is not subject to disordered desire. The text frequently adduced in support of the depravity view, one from Jeremiah, reads as follows: "The heart is deceitful above all things, and desperately wicked: who can know it?" (Jer 17:9). Very often, a second text, this one from Isaiah, is taken to buttress the preceding passage from Jeremiah: "All our righteousness are as filthy rags" (Isa 64:6). But this entire conception of human nature and action is all wrong. How often do the Scriptures speak about the upright heart, the pure heart, the good heart? How often do the Scriptures speak about deeds that are pleasing in the sight of God? These two verses are so well known because they are the exception! The overwhelming weight of Scripture runs clearly contrary to what these two verses are thought to teach. Man is born good, with the natural capacity to do what is good. This, after all, is why God commands obedience and says that he will reward those who are good and punish those who are evil. Those who become depraved become so over time through bad choices. They are not born that way. And yet, even still, made in the image of God as we are and having the law of God revealed to us through our conscience, even those who do not yet know God (or who are wicked) are capable of doing good. This is what "good people" sometimes indeed do. They exercise their capacity for natural goodness just enough to convince others that they are good. In the world, this doesn't take much, and so most people who secretly hate God are able to conceal their hatred of God. But scratch the surface of this social veneer, and the hatred of God is there.

Not incidentally, after listing all the ways in which the world's "good people" will behave badly in the last days, Paul just a few verses afterward mentions that these same people will persecute those who love God—in short, those who are true "lovers of good." As he says, "Yes, and all that will live godly in Christ Jesus shall suffer persecution" (2 Tim 3:12). These "good people" will persecute those who are lovers of God, because the lover of God reminds them of their own hatred of God. In the world, surrounded by other "good people," they can convince themselves that everything is tranquil, that nothing is amiss, that everything is as it should be, that nothing more has been required of them as a human being other than to show up to a holiday work party and be pleasant. But when the lover of God arrives on the scene, this sham goodness is exposed. The decision to try to forget about God is brought to the fore.

Once again, it must be observed that goodness is possible. The existence of goodness is not a myth, as the Augustinian doctrine of depravity would suggest. The truth is neither that everyone is a good person nor that nobody is (or can be). The truth, rather, is that genuine goodness is possible, and it exists, but it is rare. In John's Gospel, for example, when Christ speaks of the resurrection and the judgment, he explains what is to come in terms of deeds. Those who have done good deeds will inherit eternal life, while those who have done evil deeds will receive condemnation. Such is exactly what Paul himself says: "God will render to every man according to his deeds: To them who by patient continuance in well doing seek for glory and honour and immortality, eternal life: But unto them that are self-seeking and do not obey the truth, but obey unrighteousness, indignation and wrath" (Rom 2:6–8). These deeds, whether good or bad, are the expression of the heart. The good heart produces good deeds, the bad heart bad deeds. In Luke's Gospel, Christ says plainly, "A good man out of the good treasure of his heart bringeth forth that which is good; and an evil man out of the evil treasure of his heart bringeth forth that which is evil" (Luke 6:45). With these words, Christ destroys two myths at once! On one hand, the world's myth that everyone as a matter of course is a "good person," as if goodness were not truly a serious matter of the heart. On the other, the theological myth that there is no such thing as goodness at all, that there is no such thing as a good heart.

How, then, to explain the prevalence of evil if it is not in fact a fait accompli? Jude, in the course of speaking about the "last days," himself focuses on the lusts. Those who live subject to their lusts are angry to be reminded that they will be judged by God for doing so. As he says, God shall return "to execute judgment upon all, and to convince all that are ungodly among them of all their ungodly deeds which they have ungodly committed, and of all their hard speeches which ungodly sinners have spoken against him. These are murmurers, complainers, walking after their own lusts, and their mouth speaks great swelling words, having men's persons in admiration because of advantage" (Jude 15–16). Consider again the words of Paul on the matter. To be sure, he characterizes those who live away from God as evil. But it is a particular sort of evil, an evil that attempts to superficially pass itself off as good! He says that such people, "good people," are those "having a form of godliness, but denying the power thereof" (2 Tim 3:7). They are naturally able to do what is good, for the law of God is written in their hearts. And they on occasion do indeed commit good deeds. For this very reason, they condemn one another for doing evil. Again, it is possible for someone alienated from God to do good. But such good will only be intermittent, for it will lapse. This is why the apostle Peter says faith is necessary to grow in virtue, for growing in virtue is only possible by growing in godliness, and growing in godliness is only possible if one loves God, not if one only has a mere semblance of godliness. As Paul makes accordingly clear, for those who do not yet know and love God, theirs is merely a "form of godliness," for although it finds itself capable of doing what is good, it only does so apart from God. Such deeds are not wrought in God, which is why, invariably, those who live in this realm of halfway godliness also do what is evil. When the judgment of God is brought to their attention, it cuts through this veneer of godliness, exposing it as the thin, often hypocritical, goodness it is.

Presumably, our first vignette has already sufficed to illustrate the shallowness of the world's notion of goodness. But let us offer one more. It is the holiday season again, and you have returned to your childhood home. You see your parents and family. Your childhood friends, many of whom you have known for years, have returned home to see theirs. You all plan to meet up, to reminiscence about the old days, and to see what everyone is doing with their lives. You come over to one of your friend's homes, and immediately, you recognize it is not the same. It is not the same, because these friends you once knew so well, you no longer know. They are like strangers, for they have changed! The world has taken its toll on them, and though they don't tell you the specifics, you see that they have mortgaged their souls to the world. They have assumed the figure of the "good person." One of them is a photographer and lives with his girlfriend. Another is married and works for a "medicinal" marijuana dispensary. The other works in an office in the city by day, stumbling through the vicissitudes of serial monogamy by night. What separates you from them now is not so much anything particular about your life but rather the very direction it takes, for it points to eternity, not to anything in this world. And as you are now a lover of God, this means you have rejected the world's mere form of godliness. You no longer approve of fornication, so your friend with the girlfriend knows you think he should marry. As for the other friend who has, you know he is probably unfaithful—at the very least, that he still indulges in pornography. In any case, you certainly don't think selling drugs is an honorable way to make a living. And as for the other friend who has become an office worker, you needn't say a word about it, since he remembers that not too long ago he was the most critical of all of such a choice—"office drones," he used to derisively call the very kind of person he himself has since become. Your sheer presence, then, you realize, is an indictment of their lives, of what they have chosen to become. They know nothing but their lusts. No matter how kind and respectful you may be while there, you know your presence is an intrusion. How do you tell them that their life is all confusion, that everything they care so much about matters so little, that there is infinitely more to human life than becoming a photographer or an office worker? How do you tell them that life is really about living in the expectation of the fulfilment of the promise of eternal life?[2] Your entire life has become the expression of a truth they are unwilling to hear: "For God created man to be immortal, and made him to be an image of his own eternity" (Wis 1:23). But this is a truth your old friends do not want to know, and so, like Paul, you experience being made the enemy of those you know simply because you wish to tell them the truth. Perhaps, then, you say nothing. But it is still as if you did say what you didn't. For, as a lover of God, your presence reminds your old friends that they, too, must become lovers of God. But this is what they refuse to be, and so they hate you. You have become the Abel to their Cain.

In his first epistle that says so much about this love of God, this love which is absent in the lives of "good people," John speaks about the love of neighbor. In doing so, he speaks of the story of Cain and Abel. Why did Cain, who possessed merely a form of godliness, kill his brother? The murder was conceived in envy, John says. As he explains, "We should love one another, not as Cain, who was of that wicked one, and slew his brother. And wherefore slew he him? Because his own works were evil, and his brother's righteous. Marvel not, my brothers, if the world hate you" (1 John 3:11–13). To attempt to exercise one's goodness solely at one's own discretion inevitably leads to evil. For without the power of God, envy and hatred take root in the heart of the one estranged from God's love. To reject the love of God, then, is to disfigure oneself by becoming a hater of others. Rather than loving others, one loves oneself. This is the problem with lust. Your friends or your wife's coworkers may not murder you. That would be extreme. But they

2. Once again, it must be stressed, as noted in chapter 1, that living in light of the promise of eternal life does not require anything heroic or extraordinary. Aside from overt sins of the flesh, God is less concerned with what we do and more so how we do it. This was common knowledge among the earliest Christian communities of the first and second centuries AD. This mentality found its most recent and clearest historical expression in eighteenth-century Puritanism, which extolled (and hallowed) ordinary life with its notion of a vocation. As Charles Taylor says, quoting a favorite turn of phrase of the churchmen of the time, "God loveth adverbs." God, in short, cares more about how we do what we do than what we do (Taylor, *Sources of the Self*, 272–84).

must dissociate themselves from you, must banish you from their consciousness, lest the consciousness of God intrude. Although they would not dare say it, you learn that their lust matters more to them than you and your relationship do. This is because such desire is always directed toward one's own gain rather than the benefit of others. Others become mere pawns in one's attempt to satisfy one's own desire. If this means severing all ties with anyone who reminds them of this fact, that is what they will do. Because they are unable to bear the lover of God's presence, which unfurls as a "mini-eschaton," you find yourself abandoned.

In his second letter, Peter explains this parting of the ways well by emphasizing the role the looming judgment of God plays, saying, "Knowing this first, that there shall come in the last days scoffers, walking after their own lusts, and saying, Where is the promise of his coming? For since the fathers fell asleep, all things continue as they were from the beginning of the creation" (2 Pet 3:3). The life of lust—the life that displays a mere "form of godliness," the life of the "good person," the life rooted in envy and hatred—leads to lying, stealing, even murder. Such a life, however much it attempts to conceal itself, has assumed the figure of the one who came to "kill, steal, and destroy" (John 10:10). Inevitably, then, it must deny the judgment of God, the royal law of love, upon which all existence is ordained to be based. Rather than awaiting the coming of the Lord, the eventual judgment of God must be suppressed, a psychological self-deception that very often, as Peter describes, takes the form of mocking those who live faithfully in light of it. For so many generations, "good people" on the face of the earth have been living lives of lust, believing that the coming judgment of God is a sham and nothing to be feared. But Peter, who knew the Lord, cautions those who hear him not to be deceived. The judgment of God which "good people" mock is sure to come. As he says, "But, beloved, be not ignorant of this one thing, that one day is with the Lord as a thousand years, and a thousand years as one day" (2 Pet 3:8). In human terms, what appears to be a long stretch of time is as if nothing to the Lord.

What becomes of this time, this time in which the lover of God remains faithful to the law of God? Such time becomes a test, a trial. It is an examination, God's way of seeing whether you will prefer a mere form of godliness or the true godliness that finds its source in the power in him. This salvation, which takes the form of the promise, renders all that is in the world paltry.

Here, the relevance of money and riches, as both a tangible possession and a spiritual metaphor, cannot be overlooked. Quite frequently, such language is employed to express the nature of the good heart in distinction to the bad heart. To begin with, the difference turns on the matter of desire—of what is considered valuable. The good heart prizes God. As the Septuagint puts it, the good heart values the judgments of God above all else, certainly more so than money. As David says, God's commands are "to be desired more than gold, and much precious stone: sweeter also than money and the honey-comb" (Ps 18:11). Furthermore, the difference between the good heart and the bad heart is not simply a matter of divergent desire. It also leads to far different abiding conditions. Whereas the one who does good finds peace and contentment, even joy, the one who does evil remains restless, heavy with sorrow. Again refuting the theological myth of it being impossible to do good, David not only says that doing so is possible but speaks expectantly of the reward God has arranged for those who do so. As David says, peace awaits the good: "Do good, O Lord, to them that are good, and to them that are upright in heart" (Ps 124:4). And similarly, we read elsewhere in the Old Testament: "Whether a man be rich or poor, if he have a good heart toward the Lord, he shall at all times rejoice with a cheerful countenance" (Sir 26:4). When, then, it is written, "Lay up thy treasure according to the commandments of the most High, and it shall bring thee more profit than gold" (Sir 29:11), this is because "to labour, and to be content with what a man hath, is a sweet life" (Sir 40:15). Striving after what is good is itself its own reward, the greatest reward of all, for it brings us near to God, who gives us peace and joy.

In this way, everything just observed of the good heart is reversed in the case of the one who does evil. There was peace and abundance, joy and sweetness. Now there is worry and poverty, sorrow and bitterness. What had appeared to be worldly gain proves to be destitution. Such is the end forewarned to those who desire worldly things, including money, to the exclusion of desiring God. As David says in the same verse quoted above, "But them that turn aside to crooked ways the Lord will lead away with the workers of iniquity" (Ps 124:5). Rather than joy and peace, those who follow this materialistic path find only sorrow: "For of heaviness comes death, and the heaviness of the heart breaks strength" (Sir 38:18). Hence their lament when they recognize the emptiness of what they have attained: "What hath pride profited us? Or what good hath riches with our vaunting brought us?" (Wis 5:8). Forsaking God, who is our good, for the riches of this world leaves those who do so destitute. What had appeared to be wealth leads in fact into poverty instead! For spiritually, the evil heart is destitute, lacking the richness of God. Hence, as David says, the fate of those who do evil can serve as a warning of what not to become ourselves: "Behold the man who made not God his help; but trusted in the abundance of his wealth, and strengthened himself in his vanity" (Ps 52:7).[3] The true prize—the heart's true treasure—does not reside in earthly riches but in God alone.

---

3. In the verse just cited from the Septuagint, the term translated as "vanity" (ματαιότης) means emptiness, pointlessness, or futility (Bible Hub, s.v. *mataiotés*, https://biblehub.com/greek/3153.htm). Interestingly, in the King James Version, derived from the Masoretic, the one who does not seek God is described in the psalm as strengthening himself "in his wickedness" (בְּהַוָּתוֹ) rather than "in his vanity." In Hebrew, wickedness—badness, iniquity, evil—can sometimes be understood as a thing's being destroyed or broken, and hence as something that can no longer serve or fulfill its appointed function or purpose ("Wickedness"; Bible Hub, s.v. *havvah*, https://biblehub.com/hebrew/1942.htm). Take, for example, a jug that falls and is shattered into pieces. In a way, then, there is fortuitous overlap here between the phenomena of wickedness and vanity that is captured in the English (even if the underlying words in the Greek and Hebrew are different). In short, to say that someone is wicked is also to note the vanity of his situation, since, by doing evil and thus destroying himself, he has rendered his own existence pointless, empty, futile—for insofar as the point or purpose of human existence is to know and obey God, the wicked life is thus the empty and pointless one. As it is said, "For by ungodliness they destroy their lives" (Prov 1:19).

Christ, who has called everyone to eternal life, promises a new heaven and earth, wherein righteousness will dwell, where there is no more hypocrisy or disingenuousness, no more envy and hatred, but only the love of God and true love for others. This is the way opened by Christ, who himself has revealed it. How magnificent a salvation this is, that goodness should be ultimately vindicated, not in the shallow and disingenuous ways of the worldly "good person" but in the Word, the giver of all truly good things—above all, the good of eternal life, that supreme good not at all of the world.

Chapter 8

The One Who Hates His Life in This World

OF ALL THE MANY numinous and beautiful passages contained in the Psalms, perhaps it is David's hymn to God's creation in Ps 18 that shines brightest. Turning to the Septuagint, the opening verses of it read:

> The heavens declare the glory of God, and the firmament proclaims the work of his hands. Day to day utters speech, and night to night proclaims knowledge. There are no speeches or words, in which their voices are not heard. Their voice is gone out into all the earth, and their words to the ends of the world. In the sun he has set his tabernacle, and he comes forth as a bridegroom out of his chamber: he will exult as a giant to run his course. His going forth is from the extremity of heaven, and his circuit to the other end of heaven: and no one shall be hidden from his heat. (Ps 18:1–6)

However, one might think David's zetetic words[1] of praise stand in tension with the words of Paul, John, James, Peter, and

1. This particular psalm of David, which describes the motion of the sun over the earth as a circuit, figures prominently in an incredibly intriguing work

others, all of whom unambiguously disparage the world as a place of evil and darkness. How are we to reconcile the apparent contradiction between the love of creation embodied in the preceding passage from David on the one hand, and the condemnation of the world typified in the apostolic letters on the other? Or, even more fundamentally, how can it be that the lover of God, the one who loves the God who himself is love, at the same time is the one who hates the world, the very world which presumably was created by God? It all seems to be a terrible muddle, you might think! The books of the Bible, which many in our day no longer take seriously anyway, would appear not even to internally cohere. The self-confident atheist might think he could rest his case smugly right here.

But what a mistake this would be! Here, as usual, the scoffer's victory lap is much too premature. For show a little patience, dig a little deeper, and what initially may have seemed to be an obvious falsehood in fact proves to be a profound truth. As it happens, loving God is wholly compatible with loving creation, for to love creation itself is to hate the world, for the world, which is a place of human sin and evil, has disfigured creation. The heavens and the earth are beautiful, as they reveal the God who has created and sustains them. It is the world that one who loves God must hate. What, then, is the world?

To be sure, there are times when "the world" (κόσμος) is equated to creation. In such cases, the world, the cosmos, is to be understood along the lines of what we today call nature. So understood, the world signifies all the creatures and wonders God in Genesis is said to have created. A similar semantic bifurcation occurs with the notion of the flesh. At times, the flesh (σάρξ) simply designates the flesh on the bones, the skin. There is nothing pernicious or evil about skin. In other contexts, however, the same term serves as a shorthand for the evil passions. Just as the term "flesh" assumes divergent meanings depending on the context, so too with the world. When the world is condemned in statements by Christ and his disciples as being evil, the term is not intended

---

from the turn of the twentieth century titled *Terra Firma, the Earth Not a Planet: Proved from Scriptures, Reason, and Fact* (see Scott, *Terra Firma*, 140–80).

to be understood as synonymous with the creation itself—with the sun and moon, the stars, the oceans and the earth and all their creatures. Unlike Gnosticism, which condemns the visible creation as a realm of darkness and evil, the Bible teaches otherwise. The creation reveals the Word through whom it was created, as Paul states clearly in Colossians. As the opening verses to the first chapter of that letter say, "He is the image of the invisible God, the firstborn over all creation. For by him all things were created that are in heaven and that are on earth, visible and invisible, whether thrones or dominions or principalities or powers. All things were created through him and for him. And he is before all things, and in him all things consist" (Col 1:15–17). Just as Christ took on human flesh by assuming our nature, so too the whole creation is sanctified through his power. Matter is not evil, just finite and perishable, destined as it is to death, owing to the fall. As for the flesh, when it is spoken of negatively, it is solely to note the presence of what Paul calls the "evil desires" (Col 3:5) or "carnal passions" (Gal 5:19–21). It is not the skin on our bones that itself is inherently evil, only our evil deeds and desires that are committed in the flesh. This is why, in his Letter to the Romans, Paul unequivocally states that in the wake of our new birth, the body itself becomes an instrument of God's righteousness, something that would be unthinkable were it inherently evil owing to its materiality.

Taken in its negative acceptation, the world denotes a field of lust and sin. It is a place of human thought and action correlated to the evil desires of those who, despising God and his commandments, commit deeds only with the aim of self-satisfaction. For John, this domain of evil is first opened by human pride. In one's pride, one ignores God, living entirely for oneself. In turn, one's deeds are oriented by a fundamental egocentrism, an insatiable desire possessing only an eye to its own gain and gratification. For this reason, John himself likens this form of evil desire to a lust of the eyes. As he says, "Do not love the world or the things in the world. If anyone loves the world, the love of the Father is not in him. For all that is in the world—the lust of the flesh, the lust of the eyes, and the pride of life—is not of the Father but is of the world"

(1 John 2:15–16). Love not the world, says John, because it is the love of the world that blinds us to the creation, for the creation is what first of all reveals the Word. The love of the world, consisting in the prideful exercise of our lusts, alienates us from God's will. Notice how in the very next verse John stresses the transience of such lusts and what they covet: "And the world is passing away, and the lust of it; but he who does the will of God abides forever" (1 John 2:17). How else could one do the will of God but while still in the body, in the flesh? John does not disparage our corporeal condition; he does not succumb to a moral fatalism stating that it is impossible to do any good because our flesh prevents us. No, John agrees with Paul by exhorting us to use the body itself as an instrument of righteousness—which is to say, to use the body to accomplish the will of God. This is what Christ himself did as a man. We are to follow his example by orienting the flesh to carry out the purposes of the Spirit. As already mentioned, loving God entails hating the world, because hating the world means loving God by doing his will rather than giving ourselves over to the lusts leading to a life estranged from God.

Hence, what may have appeared to be an incredibly harsh, if not incoherent, statement of Christ's makes sense: "He who hates his life in this world will keep it for eternal life" (John 12:25). To hate one's life in this world does not mean hating oneself. Nor does it mean hating one's body. Nor does it mean hating others. It does not mean one is to be filled with ingratitude and anger, with sadness and despair. No! To the contrary, this is the most optimistic and life-affirming of statements! It states that we are to hate the world, because this means loving God. Loving God means doing his will, obeying the words of Christ. It is the body itself that becomes the vehicle for accomplishing the will of God, for it is through the deeds done in the body that one strives toward eternal life. The body is no longer fueled by empty lusts that merely work discontentment and sorrow. Rather, the body is empowered through the Spirit, the power to work what is good in the sight of God. In this—in this alone—lies joy and peace, all the "fruits of the Spirit," as Paul terms them in his Letter to the Galatians (Gal 5:22–23).

This vision of the human body is often expressed in the Bible's teachings about money and treasure. Money is a wage. In working, one earns money. In just this way, there is a reward, or wage, for our deeds. The wages of evil deeds are death. The wages of righteous deeds are life. What the evildoer perceives as a reward—what the lust of the eyes and the lust of the flesh provide—is thus no reward at all. For its apparent treasure is merely that—apparent. Its treasures are false gold. They are false in that they supply no lasting satisfaction. And furthermore, they are impermanent. Even if they did provide a degree of gratification that they don't, this satisfaction is in any case fleeting, for, as John says, they are "passing away" (1 John 2:17).

We have returned once again to the themes of money and possession, reward and value. As it was shown previously, gold is a metaphor for what is most to be prized in human life. Sometimes, instead, the Scriptures will simply speak of treasure or riches. Seeking God above all else is, spiritually speaking, to seek gold. For everything else other than God himself is not to be taken as the ultimate treasure. Those, then, who pursue temporal possessions rather than God in effect pursue a fool's gold, since what they esteem as absolutely valuable is not that at all. In probably the most famous stretch of text in the Bible on the subject, Christ addresses the matter directly. He says, "Lay not up for yourselves treasures upon earth, where moth and rust doth corrupt, and where thieves break through and steal: But lay up for yourselves treasures in heaven, where neither moth nor rust doth corrupt, and where thieves do not break through nor steal: For where your treasure is, there will your heart be also" (Matt 6:19–21). A few verses later, we read, "No man can serve two masters: for either he will hate the one, and love the other; or else he will hold to the one, and despise the other. Ye cannot serve God and mammon" (Matt 6:25). And then, "Take no thought, saying, What shall we eat? or, What shall we drink? or, Wherewithal shall we be clothed? [. . .] For after all these things do the Gentiles seek: for your heavenly Father knoweth that ye have need of all these things. But seek ye first the kingdom of God, and his righteousness; and all these things shall be added unto you" (Matt 6:31–33). Life, says Christ, is not about necessities such as food and clothing, nor the luxuries gold can purchase. In a word, the prize of life consists in eternal life, the incorruptible treasure not of this world awaiting those who seek it in this life, rather than all the transient things of this world.

Perhaps the most sobering illustration of someone who does not heed this wisdom is the story told of the rich man in one of Luke's parables. We are told of a rich man who finds himself in possession of a bountiful crop. Thinking of what to do with his great gain, he resolves to tear down his barns in order to construct a bigger barn to house his fruit. That night, he goes to bed, thinking about his good fortune and his future years of wealth which he assumes are his to enjoy, only instead to unexpectedly die. Alienated from God, the rich man dies poor. As the parable concludes, "So is he that layeth up treasure for himself, and is not rich toward God" (Luke 12:21). Not only is money perishable, so too are our very lives here on earth.

Why, then, did the rich man described in Luke err in the way he did? He erred, because he sought security in the wrong place. Rather than facing his mortality and looking to God for salvation, he suppressed the fear of death and, living as if he were never to die, attempted to find security in worldly possessions. In order to find God and true security, it is necessary, then, to first honestly admit to the full precariousness of life—that life itself is finite. Money provides a false comfort, an illusion that peace and security can be bought with a finite price. For this reason, admonitions against greed are common in the Scriptures. Greed is not simply a vice that warps one's character. It cuts one off from God, because it inculcates a mindset that forgets the impermanence of this temporal life. Thus, for instance, Hebrews says, "Keep your lives free from the love of money and be content with what you have, because God has said, 'Never will I leave you; never will I forsake you'" (Heb 13:5). One must keep life free of the love of money; otherwise one will lose eternal life, having instead focused solely on this temporal life. That is the lesson recurring throughout the passages considered, including Christ's words on the Sermon on the Mount.

When Christ instructs us to seek his kingdom and his righteousness first, however, there is more at work than simply cautioning us against the foolishness of greed and the desire for worldly possessions. For if one is in fact to inherit the kingdom of God, one must oneself be prepared to enter into it. The famous scene in Mark's Gospel regarding the tribute illustrates this clearly. The moment is one in which Christ teaches us that God must be worshiped, and that pursuing anything else as our absolute good, including money, is idolatry. The Herodians approach Christ, asking whether or not it is forbidden to pay tribute to Caesar. Looking at the inscription on the coin they show him, Christ rather dismissively tells them to render to Caesar what is his, and to God what is God's (Mark 12:17). What an answer! Christ does not deprecate Caesar explicitly by saying he is unworthy of tribute. He simply assigns this temporal tribute its proper place by showing that God nevertheless remains absolute. In a simple word, Christ demolishes the entire notion that the world and its kingdoms and rulers and wealth can compete with the sovereignty of God. The kingdom of heaven, and God, reigns so supremely that giving Caesar his comparatively meager due does nothing to threaten God's supremacy![2]

We are now in a position to appreciate the revolutionary spiritual teaching at work. For if it can be said that the commandments of God "bring more profit than gold" (Sir 29:11), this is ultimately because we ourselves are to become gold. The issue is one of possession. But rather than seeking to possess earthly gold, we are to let God possess us, since in dispossessing ourselves of our own wills and letting his will work through us instead, we are

2. Jacques Ellul offers a very powerful interpretation of this scene, arguing that the confrontation between the Herodians and Christ does well to illustrate that the world's kingdoms, as represented by Caesar's dominion, are under the control of Satan. Christ's words and attitudes toward money, says Ellul, are meant to suggest that we are to break free of this satanic dominion by instead prizing the kingdom of heaven above earthly kingdoms. See Ellul, *Anarchy and Christianity*, 56–70.

transformed, made ready for the kingdom of heaven. As Solomon says of those who seek their reward in God rather than anything else, "And having been a little chastised, they shall be greatly rewarded; for God proved them, and found them worthy for himself. As gold in the furnace hath he tried them and received them as a burnt offering" (Wis 2:5). Such is the lesson. That earthly life is not about seeking earthly treasure, but that one is to become the treasure by being changed into gold fit for the kingdom of heaven! No wonder, then, that Christ should tell us to seek this first, since there is no treasure that could possibly compare to it. When the inner transformation that is to take place within us is understood, then Christ's words regarding heavenly treasure make sense. Rather than storing up earthly possessions in barns, as the rich man, we are to open ourselves to God, dispossessing ourselves of everything, such that our very hearts become a storehouse, a place where God can dwell within us. It is for this reason that Christ can say, "The kingdom of heaven is within you" (Luke 18:21).

By way of conclusion, we might say a word about the figure of Demas, whom Paul in his letters mentions on three occasions. In Colossians, he is referenced by Paul in the same breath as Luke (Col 4:14). In Philemon, he is termed a "fellow worker" (Phil 1:24) in the ministry. But later, in Paul's Second Letter to Timothy, Demas has fallen from the faith, having abandoned the ministry, being a "lover of this present world" (2 Tim 4:10). How sad! Loving the things of this world, Demas inexplicably turns his back on God, and, preferring to indulge the lusts of the flesh, he spurns the promise of eternal life. The cautionary story of Demas can apply to anyone. In the last analysis, the lover of self proves to be a hater of self, for the one who hates God thereby ultimately loves his own destruction, preferring death to eternal life. If this self-destructive choice appears to make no sense, it is because it does in fact make no sense. How much better, infinitely better, to be just as Christ says—to be the one who hates his life in this world, and who thus lives life in the world but not of it. As Paul says, "I count all things but loss for the excellency of the knowledge of Christ Jesus my Lord: for whom I have suffered the loss of all things, and do count them but dung, that I may win Christ" (Phil 3:8). There could not be any starker, and more instructive, juxtaposition. Paul refined himself as gold before God by dispossessing himself of everything in this life, whereas Demas forsook God, seeking false gold in the possessions of this life. Reading of their lives now and comparing their choices, we easily see the superiority of Paul's position. He was wise, Demas foolish. As it is said, "Work your work betimes, and in his time God will give you your reward" (Sir 51:26). To return to the psalm, then, with which we began—David's hymn of creation—God's greatest work proves to be the work he makes of us if we let him refine us as gold. It falls to each of us to enact this understanding for ourselves with the time we ourselves are given.

Chapter 9

The Root of Bitterness

ALL SUFFERING TRANSFORMS US.[1] Really, it is simply a question of how so. For even along the way to eternal life, suffering is invariable. The danger, in turn, is that such suffering will lead to bitterness. And bitterness, which above all else attenuates hope, thereby has the power to destroy faith. Yes, bitterness is thus perhaps the single greatest danger along the way to eternal life, because it, more than anything else, threatens to lead the one who succumbs to it to despair and, in the pit of sorrow and the disgust of despair, to quit. For this reason, the Scriptures strenuously warn us to be vigilant against it, to be sure that we guard ourselves from the root of bitterness. For this root, if left to fester, grows weeds which have the power to choke the word of God that has been sown in the heart. In short, a bitter heart is a heart liable to lose heart altogether. Any assessment of the life of faith, then, must consider the phenomenon of bitterness carefully, in order to understand what must be done to prevent it from taking hold. How is this to be done?

To be sure, life offers numerous reasons for bitterness. Nobody is born bitter. No, bitterness is the result of time—or rather, how one has come to interpret one's present situation in time. Take

---

1. This is a theme taken up elsewhere in DeLay, *Before God*, 151–62.

The Root of Bitterness

the child. Imagine a child born into poverty with absent parents and nobody to love him in the way a child should be loved. He goes to school in ratty clothes. At lunch, he has little to eat. When the day is over, he walks home alone, because his friends are picked up by their parents but nobody at his home has a car to get him. Back at home, he shares a room with siblings. It is cold in the winter, because they have no heating; too hot in the summer, for they lack air conditioning. There are no expensive birthday presents. Sometimes, he receives hardly anything even for Christmas. Vacations are out of the question. Through these hardships and deprivations, our child understandably may be sad and anxious. He notices that he does not have what other children he knows at school have. There is fear and confusion. Perhaps there is sometimes even anger. But there is not bitterness. No, not yet.

For the root of bitterness lies in ingratitude and envy. And children are by nature disposed to gratitude, because they still are subject to the basic wonder of existence. Only the world can rob them off this wonder. Hence, it takes time for the bitterness to emerge. Imagine, then, that our poor child finishes his initial schooling. Now it is time to enter the world as an adult. His other friends have great expectations—for them, the horizon of possibilities appears boundless. But not so for him. For a long time, he had thought he would like to go to college. He was the smartest student in his class. He got the best grades, and everyone, including his teachers, praised him for his studiousness and hard work. So much potential! So our student applies to college, but for reasons we can simply imagine, he is unable to secure a scholarship. Now he will have to pay his way. He could forgo college, but his heart tells him that he must go. He wants to study history, or literature, or biology. Perhaps he wants one day to be a writer or a doctor. So he takes out student loans and heads out on his adventure, leaving his impoverished home behind. Or at least, so he thinks.

When he arrives, however, nothing has changed! To his chagrin, money is still a problem, and it is as if he still has not left home. For the weight of his past still follows him. The others in the dorms do not face the same decisions and hardships he must.

If they have credit cards, there is no worry about paying them off. Their parents do so. If they want furnishings for the living accommodations, there is no worry purchasing them. Their parents do so. If they want a new car, there is no worry buying one. Their parents do so. Everything necessary for schooling—the food, accommodations, and books—are handed to them. But he is different. He must pay for everything himself. The debt piles up, and the alienation increases. With each passing day, it becomes clearer to him that he is unlike his friends. For them, college is a time of exploration and adventure. But for him, it is a time of anxiety and stress. College has, for them, opened a capacious and expectant future, but for him, it has merely thrown him back upon a past he had hoped to forget. He cannot afford to enjoy the experience for what it is, because he is constantly burdened with worries about the future. One day, looking out his window alone in his room, our child, now a young man, ponders his situation. He compares his own situation to that of the others. He comes to see the unfairness and injustice. Society benefits the rich but burdens and exploits the poor. So much comes easily to the rich, but never to the poor. The poor, who already have less to work with, must contend with obstacles that the rich never have to conceive of. Looking out the window, thinking about his childhood, he thinks of all the things he never had, of all the experiences and joys that were never his. He sees how now, here at college, it is the same. He becomes disconsolate, convinced that nothing will change—that this is his lot in the world, in a cruel world that will always demand of him more than it does of the others who know nothing of what it is like to be poor. A dark shudder passes through his heart, and—angry at the world, frustrated at all that is stacked against him, burdened by the worry, angry at the unfairness, and envious of the lives of others—he becomes bitter. He decides that the world is unfair, that nobody cares for him. He curses God and resolves to henceforth live for himself, since everyone he knows appears to be doing the same anyway.

Very often, such bitterness is the root of the desire for worldly greatness. Of course, there are many other reasons one might strive to become great in the world. As we have seen, there is a human proclivity to desire praise, to be valued, to be recognized, to be esteemed. It certainly isn't the case that only those who grow up poor desire to one day be great. But this does happen. There are those who imagine that they will overcome their past by pressing into a glorious future. Childhood may not have been what it should, but adult life as a man in the world will compensate for all the things which they were formerly denied. Our poor child, now an ambitious young man, decides that he will be a great man. Yes, he will be a success.

Now imagine that the professor of history we had mentioned earlier is this young man, this young man who was also once a poor child. What becomes of him? Well, you say, we know what becomes of him. He is a successful, admired, influential professor of history. His colleagues esteem him. His students idolize him. His wife and children respect him. He is now comfortable financially, with all the things that as a youth he could only have dreamed of having. He now knows the abundance he had sought to attain as a college student. But you see, all this is poisoned. For the root of bitterness remains. The same envy and anger that drove him to become what he has become casts a shadow over everything that should otherwise have brought him happiness. Truth be told, he is not happy. He is simply miserable in a new way. Rather than being bitter and angry over what he does not have, he is unsatisfied with what he does have. Our successful, upper-class university professor, you see, has the same problem he did as an ambitious student. He lacks gratitude. Rather than being content with what he has, rather than seeing everything as a gift from God, he has treated life as a quest to attain what he thinks he deserves to possess. And so, he remains poor—spiritually poor, destitute of the riches that come from knowing God. This present example's details could be changed in innumerable ways. We could conceive of entirely different individuals who undergo very different events. Take, for example, one of this professor's colleagues. This other professor grew up wealthy. He was given all the things our poor professor was not. His goal in life was also to be a success, to have a career, to have a family, and to pass down the comfortable lifestyle for his children that he himself had enjoyed as a child. But time has denied him this. For, despite all his great possessions, his own son has no interest in such things. Rather than gladly receiving all the gifts the father was ready to bestow, the rich professor's son takes a different path, scorning such possessions. The son becomes a bohemian, a transient who train-hops across the country. Looking on all the things he has, this other professor is filled with bitterness, bitter at the futility of having tried to give his son what he had always thought would be his to give. Whether, then, one possesses much or little, whether one was born into much or little, these same possessions can still prove to be a root of bitterness. One professor finds them unsatisfying after having always dreamt he would be happy by final possessing them; the other finds them revolting precisely because he has been unable to give them away! However, then, one multiplies these imagined scenarios, the essential in all such cases is that bitterness with life arises over the present time and the past that has led one there—bitterness with this time that is a despairing time, because it does not live in light of the promise of eternal life.

For this reason, the Scriptures say a great deal about sorrow. The Bible does not pretend as if life is bereft of sorrow and suffering. It addresses sorrow squarely. But in doing so, it introduces a crucial distinction within such sorrow. For there is what it calls worldly sorrow, and then there is what it terms godly sorrow (2 Cor 7:10). Worldly sorrow is essentially a matter of regret. Regret over what one does not have but wishes one did have. This, in short, is covetousness. But there is also regret over what one does have but what nevertheless has failed to bring satisfaction. This, in short, is ingratitude. This is the root of worldly sorrow, a suffering whose root consists in the bitterness resulting from either wishing one had what one does not or the suffering resulting from not being satisfied with what one believed would bring one satisfaction but has not.

As for godly sorrow, it is different. And in at least two respects. To begin with, whereas worldly sorrow's regret is strictly temporal, godly sorrow suffers over the eternal. The eternal is manifest insofar as godly sorrow takes on a moral, introspective dimension that mere worldly sorrow does not. For whereas worldly sorrow pities itself by regretting what it does not have or regretting what it does have, godly sorrow no longer pities itself. It refuses to any longer pity itself, because it recognizes that the only thing truly to be regretted is what one has made of oneself. The focus, you see, is no longer on possessions or how one feels about them. The focus, instead, is on the condition of one's standing before God. In worldly sorrow, one laments over things, but in godly sorrow, one laments over oneself. Worldly sorrow still believes that if only circumstances were different, things would not be worth regretting. There would be no suffering, and hence, so it thinks, there would be no cause for sorrow. Godly sorrow, however, has finally dispensed with this illusion and recognizes that there is something deeper about life than the mere circumstances that preoccupy those who live consumed entirely with the temporal affairs of life. For godly sorrow has discovered what is most wretched of all—to not yet know God, to not yet have led the life God has truly called one to live! Where worldly sorrow breaks the spirit, godly sorrow, by contrast, is the first step toward renewing it—for godly sorrow, as Paul says, works repentance.

The preceding observations regarding bitterness indicate an ambiguity in the phenomenon necessary to address. Talk of the root of bitterness can signify two things. On the one hand, bitterness itself can be likened to a root. This, so far, is primarily what we have had in view. In this way, bitterness is itself a root, because it takes root in the heart. Once it takes root in the heart, it springs up. But is bitterness the deepest recess of the heart? Or, put another way, can the root of bitterness itself be rooted out? On the other hand, then, the root of bitterness must itself be understood to be rooted in something else—it is caused, as we have already suggested, by ingratitude or envy, among other things. What, then, has the power to root out the root of bitterness, to thereby prevent it from ever taking root altogether?

The only plausible answer is love. But not love of any sort. No, specifically the love of God. In godly sorrow, for instance, the one who regrets what he has become is not driven to despair entirely. For the experience of sorrow at issue is initiated by God's mercy. In regretting what one has become in this way—what one has made of himself and his life apart from God—there is no need for bitterness, because there is still hope. With God, things can be changed. Not all is lost. There is hope, as God in his love for us is still capable of transforming us by delivering us from the mistakes and errors that have led us to regret what we have done with our lives up to that moment. Whereas worldly sorrow breaks the one who indulges it, for such sorrow finds itself incapable of overcoming the suffering of the past or the apparent hopelessness of the future, godly sorrow renews the one who confronts it, for such sorrow finds itself capable of transcending the suffering of the past, for the future is one of hope—God, through his love, shows us we are not relegated to being what we have become. We may yet change!

It is this attitude of hope and gratitude grounded in the realization of God's mercy that explains Paul's own admirable attitude toward suffering. For Paul, although there was incredible suffering, there was not any worldly sorrow. In the immediate wake of his encounter with Christ, Paul endured the trial of godly sorrow—he faced what he had become, looked the ugly truth squarely in the face, and, clinging to God, allowed the grace of God to transform him into becoming what he had previously not striven to be. The resulting hardships along the way that God newly opened to him—the persecutions, the insults, the betrayals, and all of his other sufferings—were no occasion for regret or worldly sorrow. Paul was able to look on them with perspective in light of the promise of eternal life, a perspective enabling him to receive the good things of life with gratitude while simultaneously enduring the bad things without an attitude of anger or envy. No matter the troubles or afflictions, no matter the trials and tribulations, it is always possible to receive, like Paul, everything that unfolds with a mind of gratitude and steadfastness. Such an attitude is one that sees the events of earthly life in the light of the glory of God. As Paul accordingly says himself in his second letter to the saints at Corinth, "For which cause we faint not; but though our outward man perish, yet the inward man is renewed day by day. For our light affliction, which is but for a moment, worketh for us a far more exceeding and eternal weight of glory; While we look not at the things which are seen, but at the things which are not seen: for the things which are seen are temporal; but the things which are not seen are eternal" (2 Cor 4:15–19). The trials of this life are slight, says Paul, because one in effect can experience them now as if they were always already passed. By thinking of oneself as if already dead, one can see them clearly from the future perspective of eternity, in which they will be seen to have been nothing.[2]

Whatever suffering that takes place after undergoing the transformation of godly sorrow, thus, is quite different from the suffering and sorrow belonging to the life one knew previously. We might call this new form of sorrow a suffering that sanctifies— in short, a sanctifying sorrow. Where before worldly sorrow was owing to an ingratitude and envy leading inevitably to bitterness, here godly sorrow knows instead the suffering of persecution and injustice. Where the former sorrow did not yet know love because it did not know the love of God, this latter sorrow knows love, and thus, it learns what it means to be hated for one's love of God. One must learn to endure in love in the face of the malice and cruelty directed from those who hate God, and thus who hate those who love God. Here, suffering is a matter of hoping in God's justice. You see, in worldly sorrow, we suffer. Yet so often when this is so, we suffer only because of bad situations we ourselves

2. If this mental (and indeed spiritual) technique sounds rather akin to the ancients' "spiritual practice" or "spiritual exercise" famously attributed to them by Pierre Hadot, this is because, in following Christ, the earliest Christians were seen by others to be representatives of a new philosophy (see Hadot, *Philosophy*, 79–126). For the ancients, at least those adhering to the schools of Epicureanism, Stoicism, Platonism, or Cynicism, philosophy was a way of life, insofar as the lives of those who practiced it embodied the life of the sage responsible for founding the school in question. In the case of the Christians, Jesus is the sage. Of course, Jesus is not only a wise man but, more importantly, the Son of God, something that makes his life as a man even more worth emulating. For a very informative account of the sense in which early Christianity was itself understood to be a philosophical way of life, see Thorsteinsson, *Jesus as Philosopher*, 1–21.

have brought upon ourselves and those we know. A married man, for instance, suffers when his wife leaves him for his adultery. Or he suffers when, concealing his affair, he yearns for a full life with his mistress that he likes to imagine would be better. In both cases, to be sure, there is suffering. There is even regret and sorrow. But all this affliction is rooted in sin, which is why it leads, as it must, to bitterness. The suffering of which Paul speaks is quite different. Paul did not suffer because he has wronged others or because he has been made to endure the painful consequences of the bad decisions he has made in life. His life, characterized by so much suffering, was not plagued by the destruction of sin. No, his suffering was in a way far worse! For he was made to endure afflictions and sorrows precisely because, living in the love of God, he did not live a life of lawlessness. And for this—for his love and moral rectitude—so many of those he knew met him with hatred and evil. This, then, is true suffering, a sanctifying suffering, a suffering knowing trouble and affliction only because, having resolved itself to love, it is spurned and resented by those who themselves do not yet know the love of God, but only worldly sorrow.

Once again, here there is the danger of bitterness. For this sanctifying sorrow, it is necessary not to be bitter, not to grow angry or resentful at the injustice of its situation in this hypocritical world. Why, after all, should Paul, a genuinely good and honest man, a loving man, a man who lives a life of truth, be subject to such hatred and ugliness from others? To add insult to injury, these others who show such contempt for him, who deride him as evil, who attempt to thwart him at every pass, who belittle and mock him, who scoff at him, and who reject his message of God's love—yes, these same people are themselves so ugly and evil. How else is one to endure the manifest inversion of the situation, in which those who hate God and hate others are somehow nevertheless allowed to attack the one who, having learned godly sorrow, is truly striving to live a life of love? Is not such suffering much worse than anything our sorrowful professors had thought was too much to bear? As this sanctifying sorrow must learn, it will be possible to endure the otherwise unendurable only through what was responsible for first having converted it: it is the grace of God alone that will prove sufficient to strengthen the one who must strive against the bitterness that would otherwise take root. As the author of Hebrews explains, when facing such hypocrisy, it is necessary to look to Christ for sustenance: "To consider him that endured such contradiction of sinners against himself, lest ye be wearied and faint in your minds" (Heb 12:3). As it happens, it is very telling how often those who themselves are bitter, those who are still only consumed by merely worldly sorrow—in short, those who have a root of bitterness in their own hearts, because they do not yet know the love of God—accuse the lover of God of being bitter! After all, in the world, it is not at all uncommon to hear those who do not yet know God claim that the lover of God is the bitter one. Yes, very often, in fact, they will even go so far as to attribute the lover of God's faith to bitterness. "He is angry at the world, so he needs the fantasy of God," or "He is angry that he is not a success like us, so he compensates with all this silliness about God," or "He resents others who are better than him, so he pretends that he is really superior for believing in God." Such notions have today become commonplace for us after Nietzsche and Freud. And even if the majority of those who say such things have never read any of the works from which such ideas originate, they are still more than willing to deploy such logic when they find it convenient. What a cruel twist—that the lover of God's love of God should be explained away as bitterness by those who are themselves so bitter.

Herein lies the final temptation for the one who strives to live the life of sanctifying sorrow. One must learn what it takes to endure the false accusation of bitterness when, in fact, one's entire life is a heartfelt struggle to prevent the root of bitterness from ever taking hold of one's heart. Yes, again, what a frivolous cruelty to be mocked and derided as bitter when, in reality, one has already rooted out bitterness through love and is manifestly able to endure such cruel attacks from others only because, precisely contrary to what they say, one is not bitter at all but has already triumphed over bitterness by the grace of God. This is the paradox: to have made bitterness one's sworn enemy to such an extent that, free of it, one nevertheless is accused of bitterness by those who are themselves in the very "gall of bitterness" (Acts 8:23)! In the face of such a monstrous preposterousness, only one thing can hope to suffice: the love of God. That this should be the case is not only fitting but a source of joy. As anyone transformed by the grace of God comes to know, this power of God's love is inexhaustible, capable of sustaining us when we could not sustain ourselves. Even bitterness, ordinarily so potent, as worldly sorrow attests, is powerless against it.

Chapter 10

The Just Shall Live by Faith

WHAT POWER THE POWER of God's love is, that it not only should reveal to us the horizon of eternal life but that, in doing so, it should call us out of darkness, in turn refining us in the process, the image of God's everlasting kingdom empowering us to transform ourselves into gold fit for everlasting glory. Thus, there could not be anything further from the truth than the superficial myth, according to which the life of faith is life denying, that the desire for fellowship with God in eternal life originates in weakness and resentment, that it derives in a flight from the world as it is, as though it were the pitiable longing for an illusion. Only someone who knows virtually nothing of God (we say virtually, for it is impossible for everyone to forget God altogether)—who does not yet know the power of righteousness but remains a slave to the imaginations of his own darkened mind—could say such an untrue thing! In his second letter, the apostle Peter, for instance, who himself walked with Christ and who knew the forgiveness of Christ after having denied the Lord, characterizes the knowledge of God entirely differently than does this myth. The life of faith, in fact, is one of power. As he says, "Grace and peace be multiplied unto the knowledge of God, and of Jesus our Lord, according as his divine power hath given us all things that pertain unto life and godliness, through the knowledge of him that hath called us to glory and virtue" (2 Pet 2:2–3). In further reflecting upon the life of faith, then, let us presently consider the essential connection between righteousness and power. In short, let us consider what, as Paul says, it means for "the just to live by faith" (Rom 1:17). And as Paul's letters have a reputation for sometimes being "difficult to understand" (2 Pet 3:16), let us thus turn directly to Peter's thoughts on the subject, as they more plainly state exactly what Paul teaches also.

What, then, of the connection between righteousness and power? How is the life of faith—that is to say, the life of righteousness—the life of power? To begin with, any life can only be as glorious as its aim. And what can be greater than the aim of winning the glory of eternal life? Even those who explicitly spurn the promise of eternal life in Jesus Christ find themselves striving for a form of immortality, albeit a counterfeit one. We need look no further than to today's transhumanists, who, obsessed with the idea of transcending what they perceive to be the intolerable limits of natural man, yearn to live forever, a quest that has led them to seek a future in which man shall merge with machine—a future, in short, whereby man will no longer be man. But Christ, who himself took on the condition of man, offers us a true eternal life, if only we will submit to the way necessary to attain it. This, however, is precisely what those such as the transhumanists are unwilling to do. And so, in the confusion of their rebellion, they find themselves attempting to give to themselves what only God alone is capable of giving. By struggling to liberate themselves from the authority and ways of God, they merely reinforce God's sovereignty, since what they desire above all—eternal life—is attainable only by entering God's kingdom, not one of man's making.

For this reason, in the opening verses of the first chapter of his second letter, Peter speaks explicitly about the promises of God, specifically the promise of eternal life. As he says, God's divine power has "given unto us exceeding great and precious promises" (2 Pet 1:3), for by the commandments of God and the promise of the reward of eternal life, those who do the will of God find that they "might be partakers of the divine nature, having escaped the corruption that is in the world through lust" (2 Pet 1:4). Thus, according to Peter, God's power is in this respect at least twofold. First, it determines the conditions by which the highest end any man could seek to achieve is to be accomplished—namely, the end of attaining eternal life. And, second, in addition to determining how this end is to be achieved, it radically transforms the one who follows the path set out. For, by living as God commands, one partakes in the divine power, for God manifests himself through the Holy Spirit, in turn strengthening and empowering the one in whom he dwells.

And still, this is not all. As the next verse of Peter's letter continues, "And beside this, giving all diligence, add to your faith virtue; and to virtue knowledge" (2 Pet 1:5). Faith, which works by the love of God, does not just open the horizon to eternal life. In doing so, it transforms the very one who subjects himself to the law of God, for in keeping God's commandments, one grows in virtue and knowledge. Wisdom, which is a loving spirit, is inaccessible to a malicious and wicked heart. Only the virtuous one who has purified his heart can receive the knowledge of God, for the wisdom of God cannot dwell in the evil heart turned against God. Living by faith, hence, does not simply entail that one will thereby become virtuous. It furthermore entails that one will be wise too.

If these promises were not already enough, Peter mentions still more. In the next verse, the procession of promises continues: "And to knowledge temperance; and to temperance patience; and to patience godliness" (2 Pet 1:6). Temperance, or self-control, liberates one from evil desires. It enables one to work what is good rather than lust, the latter of which only works ruin and sorrow. The life that finds joy is thus the temperate life, the one that has learned to master its passions by desiring what is good rather than lusting after what is evil. This self-control, of course, is not confined to the immediacy of any one moment. As James says, temptation occurs, and sometimes over long durations (Jas 1:2–4, 13–15). There are extensive tests of our strength and fortitude.

These trials might unfold over days, weeks, months, or even years, thus requiring a similarly abiding commitment to what is good. Patience, thus, as Peter observes, is central to the life of faith, for it is by patience that we are able to accomplish deep works of righteousness—works coming to fruition only after long periods of striving. In other words, these works, works capable of refining our character in accordance with the good, are those that will have required of us great godliness. Temptation does not simply terminate in a periodic good act. Individual acts are, in a way, discrete, discontinuous, punctual—for each time, they are an exercise of our free will. And yet, at the same time, our actions are an expression of our character, and hence what we are predisposed to do. There is a thick, nested interrelation between act and being, between deed and being. In any case, unfolding as a continual duration, overcoming temptation is the means by which we transform our character into one pleasing to God.

By now, the inner logic determining Peter's procession of promises is clear. Far from presenting a haphazard assortment of items, Peter has explicated a process of sanctification which unfolds according to laws of eidetic necessity. For with each ensuing virtue, gift, or promise mentioned, we see that one is increasingly conforming oneself to the image of God—that is to say, is increasingly becoming more like God himself. Things begin with belief. Acknowledging God's existence is a prerequisite for beginning the path to becoming like God, for anyone who does not freely affirm God's existence will be unwilling to seek God's will in his life. It is in this act of submission to God's law revealed through Christ's commandments that one is initiated into the life of virtue. Or at least, a life of virtue that, now aided by the grace of God, leads to the expansion of one's spiritual capacities. For, as Peter says, it is through the exercise of further fruits of the Holy Spirit, such as patience and self-control, that one graduates beyond merely knowing the will of God and thereby also grows in godliness. Working what God wills, we find our very humanity sanctified as we grow in conformity to Christ.

Further explicating the logic of this spiritual progression and refinement, Peter continues, noting, "To godliness brotherly kindness; and to brotherly kindness charity" (2 Pet 1:7). If the first commandment is to love God with all of one's heart, soul, mind, and strength, then, as Peter states, it is by having fulfilled this first commandment—first by acknowledging God's existence, then by working his will in our lives—that one in turn completes the second commandant, that of loving one's neighbor. Hence, the procession of moral and spiritual promises ends in love—the love of God, and hence the love of neighbor. The entire logic of righteous existence proceeds in accord with love. Those who cannot even bring themselves to love God minimally by acknowledging his existence will never know him—which is to say, they will never know the power of the life strengthened and fulfilled by the promises of God.

Emphasizing that at stake is the matter of self-knowledge, a form of self-understanding that is at once a matter of knowing God, Peter in the next verse hastens to add, "For if these things be in you, and abound, they make you that ye shall neither be barren nor unfruitful in the knowledge of our Lord Jesus Christ" (2 Pet 1:8). Only by loving God does one know God, and only by knowing God does one come to know oneself, because only by coming to know oneself, and thus God, does one come to appreciate that the whole of existence derives its purpose from the promise of eternal life. For it is only by recognizing the promise of eternal life that one comes to appreciate how to be made in the image of God, as we are, is to have been created to know God.

It is this all-important knowledge of God which, when lacking, explains the wretchedness of the one who finds himself so situated. Peter himself likens it to a blindness. The one who is blind to God, and hence blind to his own purpose, is blind to what makes his existence what it is to be a human existence, an existence meant to find its fruition in the union with God by means of Christ, who has called each of us out of nothingness and into being. Of whoever still lacks this knowledge of God, Peter thus says, "But he that lacketh these things is blind, and cannot see afar off" (2 Pet 1:9).

And as if to emphasize that such knowledge is precious, that it is not to be taken for granted but must be cherished and protected, he quickly reminds us that even those who have found ourselves on the path to eternal life must be careful to stay on course. For, when Peter says that the one who is blind to the knowledge of God "hath forgotten that he was purged from his old sins" (2 Pet 1:9), this clearly implies that even those who have at one time known God can fall from grace. And thus, Peter concludes by noting the greatest promise of all that God promises—namely, that if one maintains oneself in the knowledge of God by growing in the Spirit, it is by doing so that one makes one's "calling and election sure: for if ye do these things, ye shall never fall" (2 Pet 1:11).

To conclude, if we comprehend Peter's words, we are positioned to see two great lies associated with the myth that the life of faith is life denying. For, if the just live by faith, it is for this same reason that they alone know power, for they, and they alone, know the power of God, for the power of God only unfolds through those who work righteousness. Hence, the very notion of a superman (*Übermensch*) who would know power supposedly by liberating himself of all constraints, and who thereby would know the will to power, turns out to be the greatest conceivable figure of human weakness. In willing a specious immortality by means of his own power, such a figure is reduced to futility. One sees this perhaps clearest of all in the fact that the very cult of false immortality, which began by criticizing the life of faith's supposed repudiation of the body, finds itself having to posit a future of humanity that will no longer even be bodily, and hence human, but instead will be synthetic, cybertronic—even, perhaps, digital. The cult of the great superman, thus, ends where all previous gnostic cults do—in the repudiation of bodily power.[1] Ironically, then, it is those who reject faith who themselves, in turn, become the great "despisers

1. See, for instance, Nick Bostrom's brief post-human manifesto, "Transhumanist Values," 3–14. Alas, in the wake of the recent proliferation of artificial intelligence, synthetic biology, and nanotechnology, such texts, though clearly deranged, can no longer be treated as the odd curiosities they once were.

of the body,"[2] for in rejecting the commandments of God, they alienate themselves from the body's greatest dignity and highest destiny: the glory of eternal life in God's everlasting kingdom.

2. Nietzsche, *Portable Nietzsche*, 146. Although it is not necessary to go into the subject here, it is worth noting that this Nietzschean expression derives from the gross misunderstanding, found in Nietzsche himself, that Christian faith, like Platonism, disdains the body. This is a terrible misrepresentation so far removed from what the Scriptures actually say about human embodiment that it is hard to believe those who propagate it are doing so in genuine ignorance.

Chapter 11

For If These Things Be in You

CONTEMPLATING THE WORD MEANS finding oneself grappling with the inexhaustible, the ineffable, and thus the essential impoverishment of one's words. There is always more to say, for no matter what or how much one says of God, it is never enough. Originating in a claim that will forever elicit them, our finite words of praise issue forth from an acknowledgment of the impossibility of their ever being able to issue a last word. In brief, praise is endless.

This boundlessness is not limited to our speech only. For the same excess that has called forth our words of praise equally solicits our deeds. The life of faith, it should be stressed, is not merely one of speech or even belief but also of action. More precisely, our very life itself assumes the form of a reply to the God who has claimed our allegiance. And for this reason, as the one who embarks upon the journey to eternal life comes to appreciate, God is always unfinished transforming us, is always further conforming us to what we are called to be in him. In the opening verses from his second letter previously mentioned, Peter says, "If these things be in you, and abound, they make you that ye shall neither be barren nor unfruitful in the knowledge of our Lord Jesus Christ" (2 Pet 1:8). To say that the precious promises of faith in God abound, thus, is to say that there is an incessant process of expansion, of growth, at work within us. For, each time we might think that God has accomplished with us what he wills, we soon realize that everything that already has been accomplished through him and in us has been a mere prelude to further change. The image of God in us endows us with a nature that is perfectible—which is to say it is only complete insofar as it continually transforms us as we press further into the pursuit of attaining a deeper conformity to the inexhaustible depths of Christ in us.

Thus, as verses 10 and 11 of the chapter in question go on to say, it is through humble perseverance that "ye shall never fall: For so an entrance shall be ministered unto you abundantly into the everlasting kingdom of our Lord and Saviour Jesus Christ" (2 Pet 1:10–11). If we have mainly discussed Peter thus far in connection with these matters, here it is now appropriate to turn our attention to Paul. When Paul, for his part, discusses this process of sanctification, he employs one of Christ's own preferred metaphors on the subject, that of likening our deeds to fruits. The idea is deep, though simple. Just as a tree is known by the fruit it bears, so too the heart is known by the deeds which come forth from it. Hence, as Paul says, the fruits of the Spirit are what display whether our life is incessantly growing in the grace responsible for producing them. In a well-known portion of his Letter to the Galatians, he accordingly lists the many good things that will be manifest in the life of the one conforming oneself to the image of God: "The fruit of the Spirit is love, joy, peace, longsuffering, gentleness, goodness, faith. Meekness, temperance: against such there is no law" (Gal 5:22–23). If these good things are all fruit constitutive of the kenotic life, it is because they emulate the very pattern of Christ's own life. For this reason, the imitatio Christi is a life that exhibits a precise inversion of the world. The world, after all, is a place of selfishness, of pride, of vanity, of greed and jealousy, of envy and deceit. It is a place wherein egocentric men, striving to attain whatever they desire for themselves, do what they see fit in order to get gain. In the verses immediately preceding his enumeration of the fruits of the Spirit, Paul had consequently begun first by listing all the various works of the flesh, the deeds committed by those who, forgetting God, live with no other law in mind other than that of pursuing what they desire for themselves.

When, then, Paul says there is no law against the deeds of the Spirit, he means to iterate what he has said elsewhere: Christ, who is the fulfillment of the law, renders possible a form of human existence that can measure up to the law of God. The advent of Christ does not absolve us of moral accountability to God. The forgiveness of past sins attained through Christ does not exonerate one to live in continued rebellion against him. The death of Christ has brought a reconciliation of man to God, because it has instituted a new covenant by which man can enter into a state of approval from God. But this covenant must be entered into freely. Even God himself cannot force one to enter into it. The trouble, of course, is that those who love their sin remain unwilling to turn to God, since that will mean giving up what they are as yet unwilling to give up. Far from slackening God's expectations of man, Christ intensifies the standard of what is to count as pleasing in God's eyes. For no longer does God merely require outward obedience to ceremonial ritual, nor even the robotic performance of moral action. Now he requires nothing short of an inner transformation in the heart, a complete and sincere renovation of the "inner man" (2 Cor 4:16). And yet, this is not such a crushing burden as it may sound! Far from driving the one who would recognize this new standard of God's covenant with man to despair,[1] God himself provides the means by which man is to fulfill it. For the virtues of the natural law—the moral law revealed to the conscience—are themselves rooted in Christ. Christ, who is the universal man, empowers those who seriously desire to conform themselves to him, giving them the power to do so. "Do not lose heart," says Paul in that same verse (2 Cor 4:16). For Christ is not a miser. As

---

1. Under the spell of an Augustinian conception of depravity, Luther himself infamously concluded that this was the case. For a more thorough critical analysis of the theological concept of original sin, as well as the doctrine of depravity that very often accompanies it, see DeLay, *Phenomenology in France*, 198–251. Additionally, for an analysis of the subject focusing on the patristics, see DeLay, *Before God*, 13–40.

Paul notes elsewhere in his Letter to the Ephesians, the glory of Christ's riches are bestowed freely to anyone who wishes to receive them: "May he grant you to be strengthened with power through his Spirit in your inner being" (Eph 3:16).

Like Peter and Paul, John, too, could not make the point any clearer when he says, "His commandments are not burdensome" (1 John 5:3). The Word, who is love and who has taken on our humanity, not only calls us to the speech of praise. Even our very deeds, which are themselves works of love, become acts of praise. This is no more unnatural or burdensome for a human heart to do than for a fig tree to bear its fruit. Goodness is nature![2] It is evil that represents a dysfunction. The theological myth that we are incapable of doing what is good, that we are incapable of pleasing God, that even so much as attempting to do so is pride or hubris— this entire set of notions runs expressly contrary to the very life of Christ, which, having set for us the example we are to follow, opens the way leading to eternal life. This, perhaps, is Christ's most radical and challenging teaching—that the heart of man is fit for divine service. If, as Paul says, the fruit of the Spirit is operative in oneself, nothing will be more obvious than that God's commandments liberate one from the pain and monotony of evil. As for those who, in defiance of Christ's words, maintain otherwise, it is only their own unwillingness to do what God has made them capable of doing that prevents them from doing so.

What an oddity—that Christ is ready to set those free who instead choose the bondage of evil. Depriving this choice of any of its apparent theological legitimacy cannot force those who believe it to see the simplicity of Christ's teaching. But we may hope that exposing it may go some way to dispelling what is a theological myth that for far too long has enjoyed a reign it never deserved.

2. As John Chrysostom says astutely, "If we are willing, virtue is very easy" (Chrysostom, *Homilies*, 93).

Chapter 12

Abide in Him

IF THERE WERE NOT the promise of eternal life openly offering itself so as to sustain the dignity of the existence of each and every human that will accept it; if we had not all been individually and collectively called into existence by a God who loves us, a God who has in turn appointed us to the hope of an eternal glory with him, and life were instead a listless waiting for death, what sadness there would then be knowing that everything, including all of human life itself, was merely a fleeting, senseless spectacle for which worldly sorrow would deserve the final word. Existence would be empty and illusory, a constant reminder (for those honest enough with themselves to admit it) that nothing true or noble ever persists. But as the one who loves God comes to understand, such despair, however prevalent among others, is only misplaced, for in working what is good and just, one can accomplish a human being's calling by participating as a co-laborer in God's restoration of creation. In short, one comes to see that one's time is not vain but rather the means by which one participates in time's redemptive goal. In this way, each of us can become an active encapsulation of creation itself, a living embodiment of God's ongoing workmanship as the project of working toward the restoration of all things continues on until all things that were once good, and are destined again to be so, shall be restored. Attempting to comprehend the colossal scale of this cosmic destiny's majesty, we are admittedly left having to resort to mere metaphor to convey what otherwise would exceed the powers of our expression completely. In trying to express such an understanding, Solomon himself says, "For the whole world before thee is as a drop of the morning dew that falleth down upon the earth" (Wis 11:22). If the whole creation itself is so slight in comparison to God, how much smaller is each of us? What a marvel, then, that God in his eternal and infinite might should enable us, through our undeniable frailty and small frame, to participate in a project of this cosmic scope. For although a mighty rain far exceeds the mass of any one of its single droplets, each retains its modest dignity, insofar as it simply is.

That the whole of creation should be condensed into the destiny of man is, of course, a former mystery now made clearly manifest in Christ. By having become as us, Christ affirms his providence over creation, for made in his image, we are thereby called to eternal life in him. We say it is Christ's creation, for, as Paul says, "By him were all things created, that are in heaven, and that are in earth, visible and invisible, whether *they be* thrones, or dominions, or principalities, or powers: all things were created by him, and for him: And he is before all things, and by him all things consist" (Col 1:16–17). And so, however apparently humble or even insignificant a given individual human existence may be, in the wake of the life, death, and resurrection of Christ, there is no excuse for despair, no reason for hopelessness, no justification for refusing to will the good. God has revealed himself, has shown us what he has called us to be by becoming like him, by following him.

This is the glory of existence. Reflecting on this glory, as Paul says in his Letter to the Romans, "Glory, honor, and peace to every man that worketh good" (Rom 2:10). Not the world's glory or the world's honor, to be sure. No, here at issue are a glory and honor capable of producing peace, joy, and hope, for such an existence is one that above all knows the love of God, having responded in love to God's own love. Quite appropriately, in the very last verse of his

Gospel, John acknowledges the impossibility of ever adequately expressing the complete inexhaustibility of God's love. Just as Christ's life on earth was itself a superabundance of good, so too it remains a marvel defying our speech's capacity to describe. John, grappling with the powerlessness of his words to state the unsayable, says of the deeds of Christ, "I suppose that even the world itself could not contain the books that should be written" (John 21:25). In the face of the excess of the Word, human words recognize their smallness.

Consequently, the only response conceivably befitting the immensity of what has encountered us is a life handing the entirety of itself over to the calling of God and his kingdom. For, in response to the gift of existence and the promise of eternal life, only love is capable of accomplishing what nothing else can, including our words. The Word responsible for eliciting our new life finds expression in this life itself, which has thus become the silent testimony to what has transformed it. Such is the power of the love of God, at once his for us and ours for him, that "such as be faithful in love shall abide with him" (Wis 3:9). Present in the truth, one experiences the deep mystery of time—that death is nothing, that the one who abides in him has nothing to fear, for one will be with Christ forever.

Bibliography

Augustine. *The Confessions*. Translated by Henry Chadwick. Oxford: Oxford World Classics, 1998.

Behrens, Georg. "Feeling of Absolute Dependence or Absolute Feeling of Dependence? (What Schleiermacher Really Said and Why It Matters)." *Religious Studies* 34 (December 1998) 471–81.

Bostrom, Nick. "Transhumanist Values." *Journal of Philosophical Research* 30 (2005) 3–14.

Brenton, Lancelot C., trans. *The Septuagint with Apocrypha: Greek and English*. Peabody, MA: Hendrickson, 1986.

Byle, Nik. *Dietrich Bonhoeffer's Christological Reinterpretation of Heidegger*. Lanham: Lexington, 2021.

Carlisle, Clare. "Kierkegaard and Heidegger." In *The Oxford Handbook of Kierkegaard*, edited by John Lippitt and George Pattison, 421–39. Oxford: Oxford University Press, 2013. https://philpapers.org/rec/CARKAH-2.

Chrétien, Jean-Louis. *Symbolique du corps: La tradition chrétienne du Cantique des Cantiques*. Paris: Presses Universitaires de France, 2005.

———. *The Unforgettable and the Unhoped For*. Translated by Jeffrey Bloechl. New York: Fordham University Press, 2002.

Chrysostom, John. *The Homilies of St. John Chrysostom on the Epistles of St. Paul to the Corinthians*. Edited by Paul A. Böer. Toledo: Veritatis Splendor, 2012.

Crowell, Steven. *Normativity and Meaning in Husserl and Heidegger*. Cambridge: Cambridge University Press, 2014.

DeLay, Steven. *Before God: Exercises in Subjectivity*. London: Rowman & Littlefield, 2020.

Bibliography

————. *In the Spirit: A Phenomenology of Faith*. Alresford: Christian Alternative, 2021.

————. *Phenomenology in France: A Philosophical and Theological Introduction*. London: Routledge, 2019.

Ellul, Jacques. *Anarchy and Christianity*. Translated by Geoffrey W. Bromiley. Eugene: Wipf & Stock, 1991.

Gramont, Jérôme de. *Le discours de la vie: Trois essais sur Platon, Kierkegaard et Nietzsche*. Paris: L'Harmattan, 2001.

Hadot, Pierre. *Philosophy as a Way of Life: Spiritual Exercises from Socrates to Foucault*. Translated by Michael Chase. Edited by Arnold I. Davidson. Oxford: Blackwell, 1995.

Heidegger, Martin. *Being and Time*. Translated by John Macquarrie and Edward Robinson. Oxford: Basil Blackwell, 1962.

————. "Phenomenology and Theology." In *Pathmarks*, edited by William McNeill, 39–62. Cambridge: Cambridge University Press, 1998.

————. "What is Metaphysics?" In *Basic Writings from "Being and Time" (1927) to "The Task of Thinking" (1964)*, edited by David Farrell Krell, 93–110. London: Routledge, 1993.

Jankélévitch, Vladimir. *Forgiveness*. Translated by Andrew Kelley. Chicago: University of Chicago Press, 2005.

Kierkegaard, Søren. *The Concept of Anxiety: A Simple Psychologically Orienting Deliberation on the Dogmatic Issue of Hereditary Sin*. Translated and edited by Reidar Thomte and Albert B. Anderson. Princeton, NJ: Princeton University Press, 1980.

Koci, Martin, and Jason W. Alvis, eds. *Transforming the Theological Turn: Phenomenology with Emmanuel Falque*. London: Rowman & Littlefield, 2020.

Lacoste, Jean-Yves. *Être en danger*. Paris: Cerf, 2011.

Marion, Jean-Luc. *D'Allieurs, la Révélation: Contribution à une historie critique et à un concept phénoménal de révélation*. Paris: Grasset, 2020.

Nietzsche, Friedrich Wilhelm. *The Portable Nietzsche*. Translated and edited by Walter Kaufmann. New York: Penguin, 1982.

————. *Thus Spoke Zarathustra: A Book for All and None*. Translated by Adrian del Carro and Robert B. Pippin. Cambridge: Cambridge University Press, 2006.

Pascal, Blaise. *Pensées*. Translated by A. Krailsheimer. New York: Penguin, 2003.

Pelagius. *Pelagius's Commentary on St Paul's Epistle to the Romans*. Translated by Theodore De Bruyn. Oxford: Clarendon, 1993.

Pippin, Robert B. *Idealism as Modernism: Hegelian Variations*. Cambridge: Cambridge University Press, 1997.

————. "Seminar 3." Heidegger's Critique of German Idealism. April 15, 2021. Zoom lecture, 2:28. https://voices.uchicago.edu/rbp1/web-video-and-web-links/.

Plato. *Gorgias*. In *Plato: Complete Works*, edited by John M. Cooper and D. S. Hutchinson, 791–869. Translated by Donald J. Zeyl. Indianapolis: Hackett, 1997.

Bibliography

————. *The Republic*. In *Plato: Complete Works*, edited by John M. Cooper and D. S. Hutchinson, 971–1223. Translated by G. M. A. Grube and C. D. C. Reeve. Indianapolis: Hackett, 1997.

Romano, Claude. *There Is: The Event and the Finitude of Appearing*. Translated by Michael B. Smith. New York: Fordham University Press, 2015.

Schopenhauer, Arthur. *Studies in Pessimism: A Series of Essays*. Translated by T. Bailey Saunders. New York: Macmillan, 1900.

Scott, David Wardlaw. *Terra Firma, the Earth Not a Planet: Proved from Scriptures, Reason, and Fact*. 1901. Facsimile of the first edition. London: Forgotten Books, 2015.

Taylor, Charles. *Sources of the Self: The Making of the Modern Identity*. Cambridge, MA: Harvard University Press, 1989.

Thorsteinsson, Runar M. *Jesus as Philosopher: The Moral Sage in the Synoptics*. Oxford: Oxford University Press, 2018.

Weil, Simone. *Gravity and Grace*. Translated by Arthur Willis. Lincoln: University of Nebraska Press, 1998.

"Wickedness, Hebrew." https://sites.google.com/site/biblecodestoday/wickedness-hebrew.